Violence and Criminal
Justice

Violence and Criminal Justice

HV
6789
.P33
1973
West

Edited by

Duncan Chappell
Battelle Law and Justice
Study Center, Seattle

John Monahan
University of California, Irvine

D.C. Heath and Company
Lexington, Massachusetts
Toronto   London

Library of Congress Cataloging in Publication Data

Pacific Northwest Conference on Violence and Criminal Justice, Issaquah,
   Wash., 1973.
   Violence and criminal justice.

   Sponsored by the Washington Criminal Justice Education and Training
Center and others.
   Includes bibliographies.
   1. Offenses against the person—United States—Congresses. 2. Violence—
United States—Congresses. 3. Criminal justice, Administration of—United
States—Congresses. I. Chappell, Duncan, ed. II. Monahan, John,
1946-   ed. III. Washington Criminal Justice Education and Training
Center. IV. Title.
HV6789.P33   1973   364.1'5'0973   74-31412
ISBN 0-669-98194-x

Published simultaneously in Canada.

Printed in the United States of America.

Paperbound International Standard Book Number: 0-669-01064-2
Clothbound International Standard Book Number: 0-669-98194-x

Library of Congress Catalog Card Number: 74-31412

Contents

List of Tables

Preface

For those Americans living in the Pacific Northwest region of the United States, the problems associated with acts of criminal violence affecting other parts of the nation have tended to appear somewhat remote. With the population scattered widely across a large geographic area—about 7 million people now reside in the states of Alaska, Idaho, Oregon, and Washington—and with few large cities, the Pacific Northwest has the lowest rate of reported violent crime among all major regions in the country.[a] As Table P-1 shows, the highest rate of violent crime is to be found on the Pacific Coast in California, followed by the Northeast region with its densely settled population.

To the "Northwesterner," living in his favored environment comprising substantial tracts of still-uncluttered wilderness and rich in natural resources, the prospect of future rapid growth and invasion by large numbers of people is viewed with increasing alarm. The explosive development being brought about in the state of Alaska following discovery of oil has provided a sharp reminder of possible aggravated social problems, including violence, on the horizon. Already, indications exist of changes in the pattern of criminal violence within the region. Table P-2 shows that over the past seven years the violent crime rate has more than doubled from 113.9 per 100,000 inhabitants in 1966 to 259.8 in 1972. Although other regions of the country have experienced similar rates of increase, the crime figures provide no grounds for complacency.

It was statistics like these that formed one of the principal catalysts for the holding of a Pacific Northwest Conference on Violence. Co-sponsored by the Washington Criminal Justice Education and Training Center and the Battelle Law and Justice Study Center, in cooperation with the Seattle Chapter of the American Psychiatric Association and the University of Washington, the conference was held on December 6-7-8, 1973, at Providence Heights, Issaquah, Washington. The conference was preceded by intensive planning undertaken by a small inter-disciplinary group from the four organizations involved in the project. It was decided in this planning phase that participation at the conference should be encouraged from throughout the Pacific Northwest region, including the Canadian province of British Columbia to make the meeting a truly regional and international gathering. It was also resolved that the attention of the conference should be focused upon particular facets of violence presenting immediate and significant problems for the criminal justice system in the region. To assist with this focus, the conference was organized around six main discussion groups—child abuse; juvenile violence; drug-induced violence; sexual violence; collective violence; and system violence. Each discussion group was to be chaired by one or more persons having special expertise in the area of concern.

[a]Violent crime is here defined according to the FBI's Uniform Crime Report classifications of murder, non-negligent manslaughter, forcible rape, robbery and aggravated assault.

Table P-1

Violent Crime in the United States, by Region

Region	Population	Violent Crime	Rate per 100,000 Inhab.
Northwest	6,706,000	17,410	259.8
Pacific	21,277,000	111,925	525.5
Mountain West	8,084,000	28,631	353.1
North Central	57,552,000	192,566	334.6
South	64,856,000	253,836	391.4
Northeast	49,757,000	223,783	449.8

Source: FBI *Uniform Crime Reports*, 1972.

Table P-2

Incidence of Violent Crime in the Northwest

	1966	1967	1968	1969	1970	1971	1972
Total Violent Crime	6,723	8,816	11,929	14,200	14,602	16,519	17,410
Rate per 100,000 Inhabitant	113.9	145.6	190.4	220.7	224.1	248.3	259.8

Source: FBI *Uniform Crime Reports*, 1966-1972.

To provide an overview and stimulus for the work of the entire conference, the planning group was extremely fortunate in attracting a group of principal speakers with national reputations and deep understanding of the problems of violence. The papers presented by these speakers at the Pacific Northwest Conference on Violence were of such quality it was felt essential to make them available to a far wider audience than the 125 conference participants who included criminal justice professionals, behavioral scientists, legislators, government administrators, and media representatives from Alaska, British Columbia, Idaho, Oregon, and Washington. We trust that this edited volume containing the conference papers will both supplement and enhance continuing debate about the serious problems of criminal violence faced by our society.

At the conference itself, the speakers whose papers are included in this volume, as well as many other distinguished discussants, spent long hours debating the issues raised. The outcomes of these discussions were a series of recommendations from each of the six discussion groups directed towards administrators and legislators. Regrettably, space precludes publication of these recommendations in full. However, among the recommendations were the following:

1. that an annual or biennial conference be held to examine continuing problems pertaining to violence and possible solutions;

2. that a commission be established to evaluate whether there should be a diagnostic study and treatment center for the violent offender;

3. that in instances of collective violence, such as occurs in prisons, the administration should be educated to negotiate during confrontation and that all negotiations should be three-way—that is, including (a) administration, (b) residents, and (c) guards;

4. that a research center for the study of criminal and self-destructive violence be established;

5. that the State of Washington develop better means for controlling the sale and accessibility of firearms;

6. that support be given for Senate Bill #2422 (federal) that would provide for a national rape center to study rape offenses and to make recommendations that will be incorporated by all the states;

7. that police receive training regarding sensitivity toward victims of sexual violence;

8. that the police officer receive training in the investigation of sexual offenses;

9. that a task force be established to study the extent of child abuse locally and nationally;

10. that in instances of child abuse, the civil rights of child and parent need to be defined;

11. that a multi-disciplinary training institution be developed for people who work with violent offenders and their victims.

It will be noticed that a significant number of the recommendations listed call for the establishment of research centers, or commissions, to examine further specific problems associated with violence. Although to date none of these recommendations has been acted upon directly by governments in the Pacific Northwest, there is no doubt that the conference has acted as a substantial spur in a number of significant and subsequent developments in the violence prevention arena. Take, for instance, the crime of forcible rape, which was the topic of much debate in the sexual violence discussion group. Since September 1973, the City of Seattle has had in place an innovative and comprehensive rape reduction project aimed at alleviating the trauma experienced by the victims of this crime, as well as enhancing the criminal justice system's enforcement and prosecution of rape laws. The attention this particular project received at the conference has almost certainly contributed to the spreading of the project's concepts to other communities both within the state of Washington and in other parts of the Pacific Northwest.

On the topic of the treatment of crime victims, and going beyond the crime of rape, the conference also stimulated substantial discussion concerning the lack of service and solicitude provided victims and witnesses throughout the criminal justice system. Following these discussions, the office of the King County Prosecutor in Seattle has begun a new program designed to meet many of these criticisms, including keeping victims of crime fully informed of the progress and outcome of the prosecutions in which they are involved.

Since the Pacific Northwest Conference on Violence, there has been a great deal of community concern expressed about the handling of violent and dangerous offenders. This concern follows the commission of a number of sensational crimes by such offenders, including a number of rape homicides by one offender who escaped from a supposedly maximum security treatment center for sexual psychopaths in the State of Washington. The diagnosis and treatment of violent and dangerous offenders represents one of the most difficult and challenging tasks confronting the contemporary criminal justice system. At a time when the emphasis is towards community-based corrections, and incarceration is increasingly limited to the most intractable and dangerous offenders, the need becomes urgent to settle upon accurate diagnostic techniques and effective treatment strategies for this group. As such, governments in the Pacific Northwest and elsewhere might well consider implementing the recommendations made by the Pacific Northwest Conference on Violence that "a commission be established to evaluate whether there should be a diagnostic study and treatment center for the violent offenders" within the region. There is much to be said in terms of cost effectiveness and efficiency for making such a commission truly Pacific Northwest in both its membership and outlook. A precedent for this regional approach to the problems of criminal violence has now been laid. It remains to be seen whether this precedent will be followed in the future.

In conclusion, as co-chairpersons of the Pacific Northwest Conference on Violence, we wish to express our warm appreciation to all those who contributed to the striking success of this pioneering effort. Especial gratitude goes to members of the interdisciplinary planning group for this conference who spent so many hours of work preparing for the three days of actual meetings. Members of this group were: Duncan Chappell, Director, Battelle Law and Justice Study Center; G. Christian Harris, M.D., psychiatrist, Chairman, Forensic Psychiatry Committee, Seattle Chapter of the American Psychiatric Association; The Honorable Judge Donald Horowitz of the King County Superior Court; Lucy Isaki, Administrative Assistant, Washington Criminal Justice Education and Training Center; James Leach, Director, Washington Criminal Justice Education and Training Center; John A. Liebert, M.D., psychiatrist, Bellevue, Washington; Hugh J. Lurie, M.D., Coordinator of Continuing Education in Psychiatry at the University of Washington; John Petrich, M.D., attending psychiatrist, King County Jail, Harborview Hospital; Lindbergh S. Sata, Department of Psychiatry, University of Washington; Dale Swenson, Superintendent, Echo Glen Children's Center; Muriel Taylor, M.D., Department of Child Psychiatry of the University of Washington. Ms. Lucy Isaki also served superbly in the role of Conference Coordinator.

In addition to the authors of the papers that appear in this volume, we also wish to thank A. Ludlow Kramer, Secretary of State, Chairman, Washington State Commission on the Causes and Prevention of Civil Disorder, for his keynote address; Professor Melvin P. Sikes of the University of Texas for his luncheon address on the psychological roots of violence; James G. Fisk of the Los Angeles Police Commission for his participation in the discussion of the subject of reducing violence in the criminal justice system; Justice Robert Utter of the Supreme Court of the State of Washington and Murray Guterson, attorney at law in the state of Washington, for leading a discussion on the subject of the victims in violence in the criminal justice system; Milton Burdman, Deputy Secretary, Washington State Department of Social and Health Services, and James Martinez of the Evergreen State College for leading discussion on the film *Attica*; Charles Z. Smith, Associate Dean of the University of Washington School of Law, for his chairing of the meetings summarizing the recommendations of the small groups; Larry Anderson, for acting as Conference Media Coordinator; and Hugh J. Lurie, for his work as a Video Tape Facility Coordinator.

Finally, we express our gratitude to the following people who so ably acted as moderators of the discussion groups in the problem areas of violence: Ralph Hirschstein, Ph.D., psychologist, Children's Orthopedic Hospital; Muriel Taylor, M.D., Department of Child Psychiatry, University of Washington; Christy N. Ulleland, M.D., Harborview Hospital, Seattle; Al Kamm, M.S.W., social worker, Children's Orthopedic Hospital; William Callahan, Superintendent, Cascadia Diagnostic Center; John A. Liebert, M.D., psychiatrist, Bellevue, Washington; John Petrich, M.D., attending psychiatrist, King County Jail, Harborview Hospital; Duncan Chappell, Ph.D., Director, Battelle Law and Justice Study Center; Jennifer James, Ph.D., Assistant Professor, Department of Psychiatry, University of Washington; Ezra Stotland, Ph.D., Director, Society and Justice Program, Professor of Psychology, University of Washington; and Dale Swenson, Superintendent, Echo Glen Children's Center.

Duncan Chappell
Director
Battelle Law and Justice
  Study Center

James Leach
Director
Washington Criminal Justice
  Education and Training Center

Note: *Washington Criminal Justice Education and Training Center* began in 1970 when a group of criminal justice administrators sought to address themselves to the urgent need for cooperation and training within and among the various disciplines in the criminal justice system. The programs offered through the Center are intended to facilitate change by drawing together diverse professional viewpoints and by providing education and training. The Center is operated by a non-profit corporation whose Board of Directors and Advisory Committee are representative of all areas of the criminal justice system. The Center has contracted with the Office of Community Development under the auspices of the Law and Justice Planning Office to bring innovative training to students throughout the State of Washington.

Battelle Law and Justice Study Center, established late in 1971, is part of the Human Affairs Research Centers (HARC) formed by Battelle Memorial Institute at Seattle to increase and focus Battelle's capabilities for scientific research and development directed toward the solution of major societal problems. The Law and Justice Study Center directs Battelle's programs in social and legal aspects of criminal and civil justice systems, and, to this end, employs a team of researchers embracing the fields of law, psychology, sociology, criminology, economics, statistics, and operations research. Battelle Memorial Institute is a not-for-profit, public-purpose, multinational organization devoted to the advancement and use of science and technology for the benefit of mankind through a broad range of research, education, and industrial development activities. It was formed in 1925 by Trustees designated by Gordon Battelle in his last will and testament, to establish a Battelle Memorial Institute as a memorial to the Battelle family. Starting with modest laboratory operations in Columbus, Ohio, it has become the world's largest, independent research organization with major laboratory facilities in Columbus; Richland, Washington; Frankfurt, Germany; and Geneva, Switzerland.

Introduction and Overview

Duncan Chappell and John Monahan

The most recent official reports tell us that violent crime in the United States has increased 59 percent in the last five years (Kelley 1973). Four of every thousand Americans, according to FBI reports, were either murdered, raped, robbed, or seriously assaulted in 1974. Forty-four percent of the entire American population now reports being afraid to walk home alone at night. Almost three times as many women (61 percent) as men (22 percent) are afraid. The elderly, the poor, and ethnic minority groups also live in an intensified climate of fear (Office of Management and Budget 1974). The growth and pervasiveness of violence has become so acute that the U.S. Attorney General recently suggested that a national police force may be on the horizon.

Data such as these led to the Pacific Northwest Conference on Violence and Criminal Justice in December of 1973—five years after the prestigious National Commission on the Causes and Prevention of Violence (Mulvihill and Tumin 1969) had issued its voluminous findings—since the need to review recent developments and to reconceptualize issues seemed pressing. The conference relied upon the major figures in the field of violence, and it sampled from the disciplines of law, criminology, psychology, and psychiatry. What took place was three days of intense learning and intellectual stimulation on both sides of the podium. This volume contains the major edited papers presented or submitted to that conference.

Marvin Wolfgang, the Director of the Center for Studies in Criminology and Criminal Law at the University of Pennsylvania, opens the volume with an overview of current perspectives in the field of violence that derives from his experience as co-director of research for the National Commission on the Causes and Prevention of Violence. Reviewing episodes of violence in ancient and medieval history, Wolfgang nonetheless concludes that violence is not an innate trait of man, as Freud and Lorenz propose, but is rather a learned response to social predicaments, especially those predicaments that constitute a "subculture of violence" (Wolfgang and Ferracuti 1967).

From his survey of crime statistics, Wolfgang demonstrates that violence is predominately a male and an urban phenomenon. His recent and classic research on crime among urban males (Wolfgang, Figlio, and Sellin 1972) followed a cohort of subjects from birth to adulthood. Wolfgang finds that over the life cycle a *majority* of urban males will have at least one contact with the criminal justice system. The importance of this finding for efforts to improve criminal justice agencies cannot be exaggerated. He also finds, however, that a small portion of the cohort (6 percent) was responsible for most of the offenses committed.

Of special relevance to those involved in correctional intervention with youth, Wolfgang notes that nearly half of those arrested for a first offense do not commit a second, and 35 percent of those who commit a second do not commit a third, with the percentage stabilizing at approximately 29 percent thereafter. This leads him to suggest that it is after the third offense that society can most efficiently maximize its treatment resources by intervening intensively with this small group of offenders. Presumably, Wolfgang is referring here to compulsory social intervention and is not questioning the value of making social and psychological services available on a voluntary basis to first and second offenders.

Wolfgang notes the increasing politicization of offenders, especially minority group offenders, that occurs in prison. He sees this as a therapeutic and constructive development because it elevates the dignity of the offender, mitigates the denegration process, and provides the impetus for leadership and service in the outside world.

Violence on an international level is the final topic considered by Wolfgang. He finds analogies between social psychological processes ingeniously demonstrated in the laboratory and the irrational escalation of conflict so often found in international relations. He ventures the optimistic predictions that personal violence will decline in the future, if for no other reason than the changing age composition of society as the "baby boom" children born after World War II grow older and thus less violence-prone. He sees an increased emphasis in the future on such economic crimes as fraud and corruption (e.g., Geis 1968).

In Chapter 2, John Monahan, an Assistant Professor in the Program in Social Ecology at the University of California, Irvine, focuses on one topic in the study of violence and the societal reaction to its occurrence: the prediction of violent acts by psychologists and psychiatrists. He surveys the pervasiveness of violence prediction in civil commitment, indeterminate sentencing, and the juvenile court. Noting the vagueness of definitions of violence, Monahan reviews the empirical literature that has attempted to validate the predictions of mental health professionals. He finds that the research has consistently demonstrated an extreme degree of overprediction. For every correct prediction of violence, there are at least two incorrect ones, and possibly many more.

The reasons for such great overprediction, Monahan argues, are several. The predictors of violence receive no feedback on the accuracy or inaccuracy of their predictions, and overpredicting violence is far less risky for the mental health professional than underpredicting it. The fact that a prediction of violence may be a prerequisite for involuntary treatment for a patient may sorely tempt a psychologist or psychiatrist to predict it just to assure the treatment. Given the illusory nature of violence predictors, the vague definitions of violence, its low base rates, and the powerlessness of those against whom predictive efforts are mounted, it is not surprising that overprediction is so extreme.

Monahan argues that many aspects of social policy deserve reinspection in view of their inability to predict violence. Indeterminate sentencing, civil commitment, early intervention programs, and preventive detention—all of which are based largely on a belief in the accuracy of violence prediction—need to be reexamined (Monahan 1975).

Monahan does not write off the task of preventing violence as hopeless, however. He proposes a shift from the study of violent-prone persons to the study of violence-eliciting situations. In this way one could attempt to modify situations, or one's response to them, or avoid such situations altogether. He presents several examples of a situational approach to violence prevention, and expresses the hope that such a change in tack will lead to gains in society's legitimate desire for self-preservation.

Seymour Halleck, Professor and Chairman of the Department of Psychiatry at the University of North Carolina, Chapel Hill, presents a multi-dimensional approach to the etiology and treatment of violent behavior in Chapter 3. He notes that the political ramifications of one's views in the area of violence have made conceptual progress very difficult (Halleck 1971).

Halleck opts for an interactional perspective on violence. Violence, he holds, is caused by the interaction of personal and environmental factors, and reliance upon one of these factors to the exclusion of the other retards understanding. Biological variables that can contribute to the etiology of violence, Halleck notes, include genetic deficits, brain dysfunctions, and physical abnormalities. Educational factors involve family and subcultural learning experiences. The environment immediately surrounding a violent act (e.g., the presence of a gun) is also a powerful determinant of violence. Finally, informational factors, such as a lack of insight into one's own motivations, can contribute to the occurrence of violence.

Surveying the field of interventions currently available to treat violent offenders, Halleck notes several generic types. Imprisonment makes it unlikely that an offender will have the opportunity to commit violent acts against the community, at least for a time. Biological modifications, such as medication and psychosurgery, have also been proposed as means to lower the probability of violence. Systematically manipulating an offender's environment to reward non-violent behavior and punish violence, as in a "token economy," is now widely employed. Techniques to reduce the environmental stress perceived by an offender, such as family therapy, may also contribute to violence reduction as may attempt to convey new information and insight to the offender.

Halleck deals directly with the ethical labyrinth confronting anyone who becomes involved in the treatment of violent persons. While he believes that the civil commitment of some emotionally disturbed persons is justified—if their condition is treatable and if their potential for violence is high—and that medication may be imposed on some persons, he opposes the use of involuntary psychosurgery, aversive conditioning, and those behavior modification programs that deny the subject basic needs and comforts. Halleck also sees a possible therapeutic and constructive outcome to the politicization and consciousness-raising process now going on in prisons.

In Chapter 4, Hans Toch, a Professor in the School of Criminal Justice at the State University of New York at Albany, argues that the criminal justice system cannot be left "holding the bag" for violence in society, since it is largely powerless to affect the social conditions that give rise to violence. Rather, Toch argues, the criminal justice system should concentrate on reducing the violence produced by its own personnel (e.g., police and prison guards). Like Halleck, Toch sees violence as a multifaceted phenomenon. One approach to its reduction emphasizes personal variables and leads to such strategies as the better screening of personnel and the dismissal of those violence-prone persons who slip through the screening. An alternate approach stresses the organizational characteristics of criminal justice agencies and results in new departmental policies to reduce excess aggression.

Toch draws on his extensive experience in reducing police violence in Oakland (Toch, Grant, and Galvin 1973) to illustrate the promise and the pitfalls of the approach he is suggesting. He especially notes the "pull of the locker room," the effects of the police peer group that often serve to stimey attempts at attitude and behavior change.

The most successful element of Toch's violence-reduction program appears to be the "Review Panel." This panel, composed of experienced police officers, confers with fellow officers who appear to be having a problem with their own violence. The aim is to promote inquiry and self-examination. Should an officer persist in a pattern of violence, other persuasive resources (e.g., police superiors) are brought in. Successful subjects become members of future panels, and a new peer group, which does not place a high value on violence, is thereby fostered.

Toch offers several prescriptions for those who would follow his lead in reducing violence by criminal justice personnel. Interventions, he suggests, must be grounded in the real life experiences of those at whom they are aimed. The sanction of those at the top of the organization must be secured, and a task orientation, rather than an amorphous reform effort, must be followed. Both the peer culture and those individuals with violence problems must be involved if the program is to be successful.

With Gilbert Geis, a Professor in the Program in Social Ecology at the University of California, Irvine, the focus of the volume shifts to the study of the victims of violence. Geis draws upon his study conducted among victims of violent crime in California who had applied for public compensation. He notes that a majority of the victims invoked the concept of offender "sickness" to reconcile their seemingly contradictory desires for revenge and compassion. Most victims, too, are not able to view themselves as entirely guiltless in their victimization, and must wrestle with the unnerving question of "Why me?"

All facets of the criminal justice system bear the wrath of the crime victim. The victim often feels—with good reason, Geis points out—that the offender fares better than he or she does. Attitudes of victims of violent crime toward the police are often favorable, with the notable exception of the victims of rape. Attitudes toward court processes, however, are almost uniformly bitter. Harassment by defense attorneys, plea bargaining by prosecutors, and the interminable delays and postponements—with the consequent loss of pay resulting from missing work in order to take part in legal proceedings that do not occur—seem designed to add insult to the already injured victim. Findings from a survey of survivors of homicide victims corroborate the conclusions drawn from the study of victims of non-lethal violence: there is "a seething and deep discontent" with those charged with the administration of justice.

Geis makes several proposals that would begin to remedy the horrendous situation he has depicted. Victims should be informed of the disposition of their case and told what the legal procedures will be. They should be thanked for their cooperation and compensated for losses suffered through court appearances and postponements, as well as compensated for any social services needed as the result of victimization. Finally, scholarly attention must be diverted to the almost ignored topic of the crime victim, if effective new programs are ever to be implemented.

In Chapter 6, Herbert Edelhertz, a Research Scientist at the Battelle Law and Justice Study Center in Seattle, compliments Geis' presentation by considering legislative efforts at compensating victims of violent crime. While compensation to crime victims was commonplace in ancient times, it has only been in the last twenty years that the modern movement to compensate crime victims has gained momentum (Edelhertz and Geis 1974).

The major reason for the lethargy in society's willingness to assume responsibility for compensating the victims of violent crime is a fiscal one. Edelhertz notes that the victim must compete with the sick and the needy for a share of the social service tax dollar. In many states, the victim is ignored by both the criminal justice and social welfare systems. This situation is rapidly changing, however, as many states have enacted victim compensation statutes and federal action in this area appears to be on the horizon.

The type of victim compensation program enacted depends in large part on the theoretical justification for the legislation. Under a social contract theory, in which the state is seen as having failed in its contract to protect citizens, benefits are seen as a matter of right. If victim compensation is seen as a form of social insurance, however, one is more likely to consider contributory fault and limits on liability, and if it is seen as welfare, a showing of financial need is likely to be a prerequisite for compensation.

Edelhertz critiques the major compensation laws now in existence. He finds some programs to be a sham (e.g., there has yet to be a payment made in the eight years the Georgia program has been in effect), and many others to have serious flaws. In general, the very poor and those with private insurance are not served by the existing compensation schemes. Like Geis, Edelhertz presents specific recommendations to advance the plight of victims. Compensation programs should have higher maximum benefits and no deductibles. They should include "pain and suffering" and exclude a test of financial needs. Together, the Geis and Edelhertz chapters outline a comprehensive and feasible approach to aid the most neglected participant in the process of criminal justice.

Duncan Chappell, the Director of the Battelle Law and Justice Study Center in Seattle, addresses a special topic in the study of violence and criminal justice—the crime of rape—in Chapter 7. The reported rape rate has doubled in the last decade, and much attention has recently been drawn to the crime of forcible rape by feminist groups who regard this area of the law as one protecting male property rights rather than a woman's bodily integrity. It is difficult, however, to know how much of the increase in the official rape rate can be attributed to an actual increase in the number of crimes committed and how much reflects an increasing tendency for women to report assaults.

Chappell points out the different definitions of rape used in different locations, with the definition in Los Angeles, for example, being much more inclusive than that in Boston. He also verifies one of the aspects of rape that raises the most furor among feminists—that is, the miniscule fraction of rapists who are ever convicted of the crime.

One of the reasons for the low conviction rate Chappell found in his in-depth study of rape in New York City is that much of the information a prosecutor would need to successfully try a rape case is never recorded. The forms on which the police report rapes are geared to property offenses, such as theft, and are not conducive to recording those details crucial to the prosecution of a rape case. On the basis of Chappell's study, new and more appropriate vehicles for reporting the crime of rape are being constructed. In addition, the New York City Police Department initiated a Rape Squad, headed by a female lieutenant, to investigate all rapes in the city and to expedite coordination between the investigation and prosecution phases of the criminal justice process.

Finally, Chappell notes the difficulty of changing juror attitudes toward the crime of rape and the dubious attempts at reducing rape rates by increasing the penalty for the offense.

In Chapter 8, James Short, the Director of the Social Research Center at Washington State University, Pullman, reviews some of the major conclusions of the National Commission on the Causes and Prevention of Violence as a prelude to his discussion of violent gangs and the criminal justice system. Short argues that gangs have changed little in the last several decades, despite much publicity to the contrary. To the extent that gangs have changed at all, it is due to the changing ecology of cities—such as the increasing availability of cars and the building of shopping centers—and the greater accessibility of guns, rather than to any political or ideological shifts. Politicization has been instigated from above, with government and foundation support, rather than from within the gangs.

On the few occasions when gangs have "gone conservative," it has generally been perceived as threatening by established political interests as well as the police. Short illustrates his thesis by references to his studies of gangs in Chicago, especially the Blackstone Rangers. It appears that the gangs are often serving as somewhat disinterested pawns in an ideological war being waged between foundations and the federal government, on the one hand, and the Chicago city government and police department, on the other (Short 1968).

Short is personally skeptical about the ability of gangs to be in the vanguard of legitimate social change. He sees gangs as "characteristically unstable" and thus unable to form the necessary political powerbase to induce change. Short fears that unless fundamental modifications are made in the causes of social unrest, the poor in general and gangs in particular will turn to organized crime as a basis for economic progress.

In the last chapter of this volume, Faith Fogarty, a bibliographer at the Battelle Law and Justice Study Center in Seattle, provides a selective bibliography of the recent literature on violence. Like the Northwest Conference, an abundance of research and written material on the cause and effects of crime occurred in response to the crime data of the sixties, and the listing here includes a representative sampling of the work published since 1969.

Several of the papers presented at the conference could not, unfortunately, be included in this volume because of space restrictions. A. Ludlow Kramer, the Secretary of State of Washington and Chairman of that state's Commission on the Causes and Prevention of Civil Disorder discussed the role of the government and the political process in the prevention and control of violent acts. Professor Melvin Sikes, of the University of Texas at Austin, considered the vagaries of definitions of violence and the history of violence against mental patients and minority groups. He focused on the violence committed by the state in the name of law enforcement as well as the violence committed on poor children through a lack of nutrition and quality education.

In reviewing the contributions to the volume, three themes appear to weave themselves through many of the chapters and to emerge as perhaps the principle issues with which the criminal justice system will be faced in the future as it attempts to cope with the dilemmas of violence. The themes are a heightened focus on the victims of violence, an increased concern with the iatrogenic violence committed in the name of criminal justice, and the possibility that the politicization of offenders may have beneficial consequences.

The movement to provide relief to victims of rape has already gained substantial momentum, as Chappell indicates, and the financial compensation to the victims of violent crime described by Edelhertz is becoming widespread. Perhaps the time is coming when the criminal justice system can face up to the more pervasive abuse of victims that Geis so poignantly depicts.

While violence committed by the criminal justice system is the explicit concern of Toch's chapter, it received treatment in many other contexts: Monahan notes the violence committed by incarcerating and treating those overpredicted to be dangerous; Short gives the example of police in Chicago dropping a member of one gang deep in another gang's territory as a form of punishment; and a policeman in Portland, Maine, was recently charged with soliciting fellow officers to form a "Death Squad" to administer summary justice to those suspected of being chronic offenders. Surely a first priority for the criminal justice system in attempting to reduce violence in society should be putting its own house in order.

Both Wolfgang and Halleck see the increased politicization and consciousness-raising currently taking place among offender populations as a potentially positive development for their own rehabilitation and for the production of social change. The ability of the criminal justice to harness this new found energy productively, rather than to perceive it as a threat and respond repressively, remains to be seen. The growing movement toward prisoners' unions might be looked at positively in this context.

As we begin the second half of the 1970s, it is becoming even more clear that drastic changes must be made in our criminal justice system, and in society as a whole, if the tide of violence is ever to abate. Crime rates cannot continue to rise as fast as they now are—an increase of one percent per month for the first half of 1974 (Saxbe 1974)—without bringing on substantial social change or massive political repression. The flight from the embattled cities to the walled suburbs is still in progress. One recent study of urban neighborhoods found that "people will tolerate a number of inadequacies in their neighborhood if they feel it is at least safe. Indeed, familiarity with events of crime and violence was the most frequently cited reason for disliking it" (Ittleson, Proshansky, Rivlin and Winkel 1974, p. 283).

The prospects for the future if violence is not contained by the criminal justice system are ominous. The success of the recent film, *Death Wish*, is an indication that a responsive chord was struck in at least a sizeable portion of the population. The protagonist is referred to as a "bleeding heart liberal," until his wife is murdered and daughter raped in their New York apartment. When the criminal justice system is unable to avenge his loss, the hero begins a vigilante campaign by walking the streets at night and killing those who attempt to mug him. Newspapers reported that the film played to packed houses and that in New York, both blacks and whites gave the hero—*their* hero—a standing ovation for his acts. Such emotions will not confine themselves to movie theaters forever. The criminal justice system must regain the trust of the people, and the reduction of violence is necessary to regain that trust.

References

Edelhertz, H. and Geis, G. 1974. *Public Compensation to Victims of Crime.* New York: Praeger.

Geis, G. 1968. *White-Collar Criminals.* New York: Atherton.

Halleck, S. 1971. *The Politics of Therapy.* New York: Science House.

Ittelson, W., Proshansky, H., Rivlin, L., and Winkel, G. 1974. *An Introduction to Environmental Psychology.* New York: Holt, Rinehart & Winston.

Monahan, J. 1975. *Community Mental Health and the Criminal Justice System.* New York: Pergamon.

Mulvihill, D. and Tumin, M., eds. 1969. *Crimes of Violence.* Washington, D.C.: U.S. Government Printing Office.

Office of Management and the Budget. 1974. *Social Indicators.* Washington, D.C.: U.S. Government Printing Office.

Saxbe, W. 1974. Quoted in R. Ostrow, "Crime Up 16 Percent in First Half of 1974," *Los Angeles Times*, October 4, p. I-6.

Short, J., ed. 1968. *Gang Delinquency and Delinquent Subcultures.* New York: Harper & Row.

Toch, H., Grant, J., and Galvin, R. 1973. *Agents of Change: A Study in Police Reform.* Cambridge, Massachusetts: Schenckman.

Wolfgang, M. and Ferrecuti, F. 1967. *The Subculture of Violence.* London: Tavistock.

Wolfgang, M., Figlio, R., and Sellin, T. 1972. *Delinquency in a Birth Cohort.* Chicago: University of Chicago Press.

**Violence and Criminal
Justice**

1 Contemporary Perspectives on Violence

Marvin Wolfgang

Much of violence is concerned with youth and the unrest of youth, and much of that unrest is the result, we are often told, of the disparity between generations. But this is not a new phenomenon as can be seen from a tablet written in Sumer around 2,000 B.C. The renowned Sumerian scholar from the University of Pennsylvania, Professor Samuel Kramer, has translated this tablet and called it the first recorded case of delinquency in Western Civilization.

The drama begins as a dialogue between a father and son, and some of it goes as follows:

"Where did you go?"
    "I didn't go anywhere."
    "If you didn't go anywhere, why do you idle about? Go to school, stand before your professor; recite your assignment, open your school bag; write in your tablet; let your big brother write your new tablet for you; and then report to your monitor. Do not wander about the streets. Come now, be a man, don't stand about in the public square or wander about the boulevard and when walking in the street, be humble; don't look all around. Show some fear before your monitor. Go to school. It will benefit you. Night and day I am tortured because of you. Night and day you waste in pleasures; you have accumulated some wealth and expanded far and wide; you have become fat, big, broad, powerful and puffed but your kin waits expectantly for your misfortune and we will rejoice at it because you look not to your humanity."

Then later on, the father says to himself in a kind of soliloquy:

"He is beaten by a God; he is criminal; he is a robber; he breaks into houses. He is a slanderer; he stinks. He is a fool, a wild man, a driveling person—neglects everything. He is weak—he smells bad. He is crazy; he is thinking food. His body is marked by disease; he says evil things and he is an informer."

The Sumerian tablets go on that way for quite a long while, but I think we might do well to recall the message of this one lest we become too enamored or too disturbed about our own rebellious and sometimes violent youth.

There is one other historical reference to be made. In 1343, when the dictatorial Duke of Athens in Florence was compelled by an angry mob to flee that city, some of his political assistants were grabbed on the street, tortured, and murdered. The apex of the mob fury—collective violence—reached in that scene was described by Machiavelli:

1

Those who could not wound them while alive, wounded them after they were dead and not satisfied with tearing them to pieces, they hewed their bodies with swords, tore them with their hands and even with their teeth, and that every sense might be satiated with vengeance having first heard their moans, seen their wounds and touched their lacerated bodies, they wished even the stomach to be satisfied—that having glutted the external sense the one within might also have its share.

That is pretty violent stuff and may sometimes make our urban riots seem not quite so bad. This mob action helped to sustain Machiavelli's insistence that the rage of men is certainly always greater and their revenge more furious upon the recovery of liberty, than when it has only been defended.

The reason for referring to this scene is probably obvious: to draw upon an example of rioting and violence in a beautiful city at the most glorious time in its history in order to show that the brutal side of man's behavior in the midst of another period's affluence, political enlightenment, and highly humanistic culture did exist. Man is not innately criminal, however, nor is he innately violent or aggressive. He responds to people, to events or other kinds of stimuli that precipitate violent or aggressive behavior. He learns what is fearful or frustrating so that the things to which he reacts are interpreted by him as such and the resolution of events that he defines as problems is also learned. Cats, dogs, and monkeys do not shoot their adversaries because they cannot or have not learned to use guns. Only man has the capacity to make and to use such artificial weapons designed to destroy himself and others.

Violence has many meanings. I learned in one of my first trips to Israel that the word for violence in Hebrew has the same etymological root as the word for "mute," and I have on more than one occasion drawn upon that interesting similarity of derivation. In one sense, the resort to violence suggests that one does not have an adequate repertoire of other kinds of responses to frustrating, difficult situations; in another sense, the root word can be applied to man's capacity to cope with his environment. Violence—so far as I, as a sociologist, am concerned—is learned behavior. Most of my colleagues in my discipline reject the notion of aggressivity as having a kind of Freudian instinctive character, and in most cases, I would clash with Konrad Lorenz's expressions about the virtual innate character of man's violence.

Violence is a term we struggled a great deal with in the Violence Commission. Essentially we spoke of it as an infliction of injury on a body or property of others. But this certainly is not a completely satisfying, totally comprehensive definition. We know that there are crimes of violence, and these were easily handled by our definitions. But there are other kinds of violence that deal with violence on the highways and violence with guns; there is legitimized violence that is committed by persons in legitimate authority. Simply cataloging such episodes as Kent State and Attica and Vietnam or executions performed by the state reveal the character of what is meant by violence performed by legitimate authorities. The political violence that exists in the world is another form. Senator Robert Kennedy, shortly before the Commission was established and before his assassination, referred to the violence that is committed on miners' lungs as they reach into the bowels of the earth. There is also an enormous amount of violence indirectly committed by the way our political and economic systems function. The gnawing at infants' toes by rats in the ghettos of our cities may be viewed as a form of violence.

Within a five-year period, from 1966 to 1971, there was an increase of nearly 90 percent in the number of violent crimes committed in the United States; in terms of rates per 100,000, the increase was 50 percent for murder, 55 percent for rape, 49 percent for aggravated assault. These crime frequencies are collected by the FBI from police departments across the country and undoubtedly include underestimates since many crimes are unreported to the police for such reasons as fear or hopelessness on the part of the victim. The problem of ill-reporting is perhaps one that we might take up in this discussion for we know from sample victim surveys that there is a considerable unreporting of even the serious crimes of violence.

It is certainly a fact that violence occurs more in our cities than in country or rural regions. In 1971, for example, for cities of at least 250,000, the homicide rate was 19 compared with the rural rate of 7. The urban rape rate was 44 compared with the rural rate of 11. And the comparative rate for assaults were 351 in the city, 101 in the rural areas.

Another recognized fact about these crimes of violence is that the crime frequency in the United States—and here we are dealing mostly with an urban phenomenon—is associated with economic class and race of both the victim and the offender. In cases of assaultive crimes against persons, the black offender rate in large cities is substantially higher than the white rate. In a recent *New York Times* survey (in August of 1973), it was noted that 60 percent of those arrested for homicide were black, 25 percent were Hispanic, and 15 percent white. It is also evident that the rate of assault against Negro victims by Negro offenders is far higher than the rate against white victims by Negro offenders. And in that same *New York Times* survey, 9 percent of the homicides for which blacks were arrested involved white victims, while 48 percent of the homicides for which blacks were arrested involved black victims.

According to an earlier national survey, which was conducted by the President's Crime Commission in 1967, the rate of assault on blacks by black offenders was almost 3,000 per 100,000, while the white victim rate by black offenders was only 175. So while it is true that blacks commit assaultive and other crimes at a higher rate than whites, the larger proportion of these crimes is directed against other blacks; the higher frequency of black crime is then mostly an intraracial phenomenon.

With respect to economic class, unquestionably the crime rate among members of the poorest class, whether black or white, is many times higher than the working- or middle-class rate.

Another fact that we must keep in mind is that violence is exhibited predominantly by the male of the species. Again according to that *New York Times* survey, 87 percent of those arrested for homicides in New York, during 1971, were males. Rapes, assaults, street robberies, burglaries as well as all kinds and degrees of homicide are, to all intents and purposes, male phenomena.

As is typically the case, the more deeply one becomes involved in a particular kind of study or phenomenon, the more one is likely to admit ignorance or the inability to provide explanations and derive solutions. Accordingly, the explanations for violence are legion: poverty, ill education, poor parental supervision, the XYY, machismo, guns, urban density, youth, and males. These variables are almost always co-related in any study of violence on any grand scale, and in the aggregate, they cannot be denied.

I have indeed called the existence of a great deal of urban violence "subcultural violence." This thesis refers to the fact that congested groups of people share a belief system, a value system, and a set of attitudes and habits concerning the ready resort to violence in a setting where violence is indeed not only tolerated but often encouraged and sometimes required in certain kinds of interpersonal situations. The thesis, however, does not explain the presence of violence. It does not say very much about the etiology, or origin of violence, and therefore, like most theses, it stands in some posture of vulnerability and limitation. But I am convinced of the value of pursuing further investigation of the notion of a subculture of violence in an interdisciplinary way.

One of the things that we are all interested in doing, whether we are in academia or administering criminal justice programs or superintending a correctional institution, is to predict violence. But that perhaps is even more difficult than explaining the existence of violence. The difficulties of predicting violent behavior even among a small and limited set of persons released on parole, preclude efforts to attain much accuracy or efficiency beyond the operation of chance. When the universe from which violent behavior is to be predicted comprises offenders arrested or convicted for the first time or, even worse, an entire population with or without criminal records, the problems of prediction are compounded. Anyone who asserts that science has the tools to predict violent criminal behavior from the population at large has not adequately considered the problems of computing mathematical probabilities, or has not taken into account the imprecision of our diagnostic instruments or even the consequences of the invasion of privacy if psychiatric and psychological tests were to be given to the entire population for this purpose. The infrequency of recorded instances of criminality, and particularly of criminally violent behavior, is such that it produces an enormous number of false positives in trying to predict because of the propensity of overprediction. The number of civil rights denials, because of false positives leading to intervention by society before crime occurs, would be staggering.

As a sociologist, I am impressed by the physio-biological and biochemical approaches to the study of human behavior. I am impressed with the work of men like Delgado, Frank Ervin, Vernon Marks—who have used electrical stimulation of brain cells and drug therapy for aggressive and hostile patients. The works are fascinating and may eventually lead to the better understanding and control and treatment of violent behavior.

The XYY gene structure of some homicide offenders awaiting trial or already in prison is biological news. But there is yet no information about the distribution of XYY in the general population or about the probability of XYYs violating the law, committing aggressive crimes, or becoming lawyers or judges. I am reminded that in 1928 a book by Schlapp and Smith was called *The New Criminology* in which reference was made to break-through knowledge about the relationships between the pituitary and thyroid glands and robbery, murder, and theft. They had very neat tables showing direct correlations. I am also reminded of Gall and Spurzheim with their term "craniology" in the nineteenth century, of William Sheldon's "constitutional psychiatry," as well as of the failures of the father of scientific study of criminology, Lombroso, on physiognomy and criminal anthropology.

I am not denying the fact that knowing the gene structure and the physiological, sociological, and psychiatric variables and attributes of persons who are convicted and sentenced to prison may be useful for purposes of classification or for designing experimental studies, but I am reluctant to suggest that we are anywhere near the threshold of being able to predict with any of those variables.

The public impression seems to be that medical scientists tend to make mistakes in the direction of freeing violence-prone persons who later become "raving maniacs." I am referring to a recent *Medical World News Report* in which the author pointed this out by reminding us that Charles Whitman, who shot 41 people from a tower in Texas and killed 17, had been consulting a psychiatrist before he went on his shooting spree, and that last year in California, Emil Kemper, III, who had shot his grandmother in 1964 and who was deemed by two court-appointed psychiatrists as no longer any danger to society, murdered his mother and one of her friends as well as six young girls just one year after his release.

As the author of this *Medical World News Report* notes, the evidence indicates that psychiatrists, however, generally make mistakes on the side of excessive caution and detain too many people who are really innocuous. One may disagree with this assertion, but it does point to a reference of Henry Steedman at the Mental Health Research Department in the New York State Department of Mental Hygiene who referred to a study of 400 New York mental patients who had been classified as "extremely dangerous" by psychiatrists and hospitalized for long periods. Several years afterwards, the patients were released and only 17 percent were re-arrested. Dr. Douglas Sargent of the College of Osteopathic Medicine in Michigan has said that "we have not advanced beyond the level of descriptive study," and I am inclined to agree. We simply do not have that precision in our descriptive interpretation of violence. We have it sometimes after the fact but not before the fact. I suggest that stage between acts is probably the point of maximum efficiency and economy in prediction pay-off, that once an offender has committed a crime of violence, the probability matrix that can be produced—background factors, type of offense, conduct in prison—may eventually be of sufficient validity to permit its being utilized as a model for decision making about therapy and about sentence disposition by the judiciary. When troubled people become visible to those in the healing arts and those who administer the law, there is some chance—as well as the social right—to diagnose and subject them to examinations and tests to classify their behavior and to intervene. I am suggesting that social intervention occur only after we have already seen a display of troubled behavior. The display of certain kinds of aggressivity may indeed be the best indicator of other and much more serious kinds. Graduation and gravity of criminality is still an inadequately researched topic, but the best lead to predictions success would appear to lie in this focal issue.

Finally on this point, again as a sociologist, I assert that a medical model of illness and case methodology has not and is not likely to explain crime in general or violent criminality. Crime or deviance is conduct that is defined by culture and values, and social relationships are systems of belief and interactions that are learned and incorporated into the personality structure. Crimes of violence, I state again, are learned responses. But that there is an uneven distribution of such crimes throughout the population is an enormous clue to the sociology of understanding such conduct.

Along these same lines about waiting until an act is committed, I should like to refer to a study that I have been involved in at our Center for Studies in Criminology and Criminal Law, which we call a "birth cohort" (*Delinquency in a Birth Cohort*, University of Chicago Press, 1972). From that study of a birth cohort, it is clear that there is a relatively small cadre of people who are committing violent crimes and violence in general.

The birth cohort study in Philadelphia is a unique collection of information. We took approximately 10,000 boys (mainly because violence is primarily a male phenomena) born in 1945 who lived in Philadelphia while they were at least 10 to 18 years old. They constituted a group all born at the same time and whom we followed longitudinally up to age 18. (We have, incidentally, subsequently interviewed a 10 percent sample of them and have now followed them up to age 26 in what seems to be one of those studies in which a criminologist/sociologist can make a career out of studying the same group.)

From the entire cohort, 35 percent were found delinquent, which means that they had at least one contact with the police before reaching age 18. I recognize all the problems of criminal statistics and the fact that we are talking about the official recording by the police. In one sense, then, the best phrase to use is that

35 percent of them were "caught in the network of the juvenile justice system." While we recognized that there may be differential handling of juveniles by the police and that there is a lot of hidden delinquency, the finding of 35 percent delinquent was startling to us because previous statistics suggested that only about 2 percent get into trouble with the law or perhaps in the ghettos, about 5 percent are delinquent. But if one waits long enough, one can accumulate up to 35 percent delinquent by age 18, and I can now report that up to age 26, we have accumulated another 10 percent. Thus, I am sure that if we go through the whole life cycle of a birth cohort, we will go well over 50 percent who have had at least one arrest.

About 29 percent of the white boys and more than 50 percent of the black boys in our cohort were delinquent. It is a startling and interesting fact that a black boy in a large urban community has more than a 50 percent chance of being arrested by the police before he reaches 18. It is a dramatic and disturbing fact. Of special significance is the fact that only 627 boys out of the entire cohort of 10,000 were classified as chronic offenders—that is, they committed five or more offenses or, perhaps more properly, were picked up by the police five or more times during their juvenile court ages. These chronic offenders represent only around 6 percent of the entire birth cohort and 18 percent of the delinquent group; yet, this small group of 627 were responsible for 5,300 delinquencies, or 52 percent of all such acts committed by the entire birth cohort. They were heavily represented among those who committed violent offenses; about 55 percent of all the offenses we designated violent were committed by this small group of 627. They were responsible for 71 percent of the robberies and for all the homicides. The other offenses committed by most of the other delinquents in the birth cohort were relatively trivial, and when we tried to grade them (i.e., weight them in some way by a seriousness score that we had worked out earlier), the differences between the hard core—the chronic small group of 627—and the others became even more dramatic.

There is one other point about the birth cohort deserving mention: when we examined the number of offenses committed over a period of time and followed them out to 15 offenses, we found that 47 percent—that is, nearly half—of the boys stopped after the first offense. Most of their offenses were relatively trivial, and it would be wasteful, inefficient, and uneconomical for society to spend much, if any, time with juveniles who commit their first offense unless that offense is a very serious one.

About 35 percent stopped after their second offense and never went on to a third; after the third offense, about 29 percent stopped. The same percentage followed throughout the rest of the incidents—that is, about 29 percent, stopped after each additional offense. Stability occurring after the third offense led us to suggest that point—after the third offense—for society to maximize the efficiency of its talent, time, and resources by intervening then—intensively—with that small group at that time.

I would also like to address the problem of neutralization and politicization relative to violence. Youth do not reflect their older generation's problems so much as react to them. Their reaction is in part a rejection of the problems that those in the establishment have created, perpetuated, or not solved, and the rejection may take the form of tolerated deviancy or untolerated crime and violence. An attack on the social order, whether by cheating the telephone company, shoplifting from major chain stores, or bombing the Bank of America, becomes a political act neutralized from its guilt-causing mechanism because of the corruption assumed to lie within the system. The traditional, common-law youthful offender of many generations previously had much of this same kind of attitude, more nascent in its politicality but nonetheless felt. Today, as never before, this assumed ideological legitimacy is persuading and pervading youth in great numbers everywhere. The delinquent gang is not a collection of mental pathology but rather a somewhat and sometimes organized group seeking to compensate for the exploitation and reduced life opportunities suffered by them, their parents, and their grandparents. The prostitute always laughs at the hypocrisy of sex in the straight society and yet ultimately wishes to join it. Organized crime is in one sense a more congenial and systematic reflection of this same attitude of making ridiculous, by its blatancy, the inherent corruption of the larger culture in which such crimes can function.

This form of politicization has developed in the United States but has not yet been systematically analyzed by criminologists. Both on the street and in prison, there is evidence that this development is most prevalent among blacks. I refer to a generalized mind set that uses criminal assaults on white persons and property as compensatory, justifiable behavior.

Eldridge Cleaver probably expressed this position most clearly in *Soul on Ice* when he spoke about rape:

A slave who dies of natural causes, cannot balance two dead flies in the scale of eternity. It delighted me that I was defying and trampling on white men's law, upon his system of values. I felt I was getting revenge. I wanted to send waves of consternation throughout the white race. I know that if I had not been apprehended I would have slit some white throats. There are, of course, many young blacks out there right now, who are slitting white throats and raping the white girls.

From my discussions with young blacks, I doubt that most have read Cleaver, but there has been a systemic diffusion among them of this philosophy. Ripping-off white property and white men and women is viewed as compensation for disadvantage, lack of opportunity, and thereby contains neutralization of guilt. Interracial attacks have increased and can be expected in a social transition toward equality. It is fearsome, of course, for whites to see potential threat to their safety, and so long as repression is the ostensible solution, this form of politicization will be viewed as dysfunctional and destructive but, I suggest, will continue and increase.

We are now witnessing a new phenomenon in our prisons, which we still euphemistically call "correctional" institutions. Young men and women who may have committed crimes as individuals and with little cognizant awareness of why they did are incarcerated with others of like background. But instead of becoming highly prisonized and taking on the old roles of prisoners of yesteryear—the loner, the Rat Fink, the wolf, the con man, the square John, and so forth—they now collectivize around a new political ideology. No longer willing to become mechanical automatons doing time and more concerned with their political and emotional health than with getting out only to be returned to their same despairing environment, they have become politicized and rally around the attack, not only on the correctional system but the entire social system that victimized them in the first place. Their previously designated idiosyncracy in psychopathology becomes transformed into a politically meaningful behavior for them when shared by the inmates into whose propinquity they have been placed. Madness and the sick label are thrown off for the more palatable designation of radical. I suppose they concur with F. Scott Fitzgerald who said: "When the world changes from the good and bad to the sick and the well, I'd rather be dead." Moreover, they no longer see themselves as bad, let alone sick.

This form of politicization is occurring mostly among black inmates in prison. I believe it to be essentially therapeutic for prisoners and constructive for society. Offenders who violated the law as individuals or as amorphous advocates with individualistic concern for some economic or psychological gain through burglary, robbery, or similar acts, become politically conscious in prison because of the new form of inmate culture. Blacks numerically dominate many of our urban state and federal prisons, and these blacks have become organized by religion, ethnicity, and politics against the higher prevailing social system. Their grievances have begun to rise above, but may include, the prison administration and guard system, meals, and privileges in prison. The new arrivals are quickly socialized by the black politicals—the Moslems, the Communists, the Panthers— and transfer their streetwise intelligence and coping resourcefulness into group politics and collective consciousness. I am aware that there are similar phenomena occurring in other countries, but in the United States, unionization and politicization, which are two different things, are mostly among the black minority.

This activity is therapeutic and constructive because the groups have elevated the dignity of the individual; they have reduced the denigration process and have functioned productively in an indigenous style to aid released offenders to succeed in the community with an ethos of service and leadership that parallels the political boss and ward leader of an earlier era for the Irish and the Italians, particularly, in American local politics. I don't know where and how far this kind of prisoner politicization will lead, but the prognosis looks good. Recent prison riots have been violent pangs of birth of this phenomenon, but much more extensive are the elements of growth throughout the country. The rights to be treated, not to be treated, or to treat one's self are being thrust upon correctional administrations that cannot ignore such claims. And criminologists are joining—or will join—these criminals not in romantic affiliation with a kind of colonial superordinate attitude burdened with helping but in becoming politicized themselves and seeing the values and virtues of a political conscious-ness as a group therapeutic process where psychiatric group therapy has failed.

There is another feature of our culture that I think has unwittingly produced confusion and conflict between youth and the older generation and therefore has stimulated some unrest and frustration, even perhaps rebellious, riotous, and sometimes violent behavior. There is a sado masochistic component of our social interactions that ranges from personal to international relationships. I am not prepared to suggest what might be done about this feature nor that I am even describing it accurately, but I suggest that it exists and forms a basis for conflict.

On the interpersonal level, sex is probably the most clear example. In each sex encounter, the one partner seeks his own satisfaction in a moment of supreme selfishness and inevitably holds the other in a subject-object relation-ship. This is not a male-female, dominant-submissive relationship; rather, it is at once promoting the painful relationship of using the other in a sexual relationship and of withholding, even in release and essence, elements known only to self. Investment of self is contingent on self-gratifications and satisfac-tions, whether to produce ecstasy in self or in other or in both. Yet self must be turned over to the other; self must be an object for the thrust and reward for the other. We allow an enormous essence of our own existence to be drawn from us, to be used as object and the reverse in the object-subject drama. The self is subjected to the slavery of the senses of another. In our own self-indulgence, we submit and yield. That there is romantic symbiosis in much of this does not deny the validity of taking from one another or giving up one's self.

Jean Paul Sartre has poignantly referred to this interaction as at once sadism and masochism. No marriage manual speaks in these terms. We are told instead about the mystical quality of natural and simultaneous glorification of the act of love, which is both a statistical infrequency and an exploitation of mythical illusions. But the youth of today are telling us about freedom and the absurdity of sexual myths. They are unsure but searching for the reality of giving and receiving and in recognizing that the escalation of sexual investment unencum-bered by other commitments can be rewarding in itself—that is, the romance of forever or a pecuniary transaction can be equal. Unconditional acceptance in a love act requires no self-evasing moves, no target for aggression, no investment of one's history, and no concern about the invasion of one's personal territory. Sex in the culture of many youths today is a recognized yielding and a fulfilling seeking as well as an awareness of the character and quality of the interpersonal dyad. I think this awareness in itself makes the entire drama unthreatening to both partners, but the older generation remains fixed in an institutional mode and views youthful sex as promiscuous or ephemeral, uncommitted transiency, sensation without intimacy. Some unrest comes from a desire to retreat from the compromising conditional accommodations of this old sado masochistic character of much existing sex.

Let me move directly to international relations that reflect the amount of violence we have experienced in this country. It is here that sham and poker playing with men's lives are perhaps the most blatant and most disturbing to youth everywhere. From a dyad to national conflict, there is a process described by a colleague of mine, psychologist Allan Teeger, that is quite similar. First, the parties enter into conflict. With each assuming the ability to obtain victory—which goal is more valuable than resources, money, men, time, energy, ego increase and so forth—and with each expending resources without the capacity to recover them, the goal in the conflict becomes that of breaking even on the expenses. This is victory in order to reduce losses. Each side in the dispute has by now put so much into the conflict situation that retreat means no victory of the original prize but total loss of all investments. You might think of the present administrators and administrations having this kind of conflict confrontation with the prisoner population. After the first stage, the goal of making a profit shifts to the second stage in the interaction—when an attempt to minimize losses is made—since losses now exceed the benefits of the initial goal. Then a third stage, a third goal, occurs; namely, inflicting harm on the opponent simply for the sake of harm—to beat the other person, or group, or nation, whatever the cost. When this decision is reached in the escalation of the interaction, it is generally with the assumption that whatever costs are involved can be justified. But over time, it becomes obvious to both parties that there can be no real winner and loser. That these terms become meaningless and with this goal out of reach, a new decision and a new goal is commonly made—that of saving face. Saving face and fear of losing face become identical concepts. This is a war of attrition and the conflict remains stable or ends simply because the parties have no resources remaining to continue the conflict.

Dr. Teeger describes this kind of phenomenon in a research program that uses a classroom demonstration of escalation of conflict. The experimenter auctions off a dollar to the highest bidder. The winner—the person with the highest bid—pays his bid according to the rules of the game and receives the dollar prize. The class is told in advance that this auction is a bit different from the usual auction in that not only will the winner pay his bid and receive a dollar bill but the second highest bidder will pay his bid also but receive nothing. Although many students enter into the bidding initially, usually all but two drop out as the bidding approached the dollar mark; the rest are afraid of being the second highest bidder and therefore losing their bids.

In this example, let us imagine that person "A" has bid 80¢ and person "B" bid 90¢, which is indeed what has happened many times in the experiment. If "A" quits at this point, he will lose his 80¢ and receive nothing, for he would be the second highest bidder. "B" would be the winner paying 90¢ and receiving a dollar in return. However, "A" might chose to increase his bid to $1.00 and thus avoid the certain loss of 80¢ if he quits. "B" is now faced with the choice of quitting and losing 90¢ or increasing his bid to $1.10; he knows full well that if he chooses to bid $1.10, becoming the winner at this point would only cost 10¢ rather than the total amount of his second-place bid. Now the process continues, of course, with each player increasing his bid in an attempt to be the winner, and there is no rational solution.

Each small increase is justified, for it is worth the risk of losing an additional ten cents rather than accepting the certain loss of all that you have already bid. Thus, in the short run, it is rational to continue to bid; in the long run, it is irrational. Whenever this demonstration has been attempted, the bids always exceeded $1.00 and have gone as high as $10.00. The demonstration has been conducted successfully with undergraduates in many classes as well as with graduate students in psychology, political science, sociology, and psychology faculty members, some of whom were very experienced in game theory and conflict.

Thus, in a situation in which the value of victory is fixed and in which both parties to the conflict will lose all that they have invested in the conflict, it is possible to reach a point where investments of each party equal the value of victory. When faced with this situation, the inevitable result appears to be that the parties to the conflict choose to extend the conflict rather than accept their loss. The winner, therefore, will always pay more for victory than it is worth.

How do these descriptions of conflict situations affect the unrest of much of our population and violence? In several ways, I think. First, unlike the unconditional surrender of World War II, the Korean and Vietnam combat actions found that the original goals of victory were substituted by face-saving goals. Almost every analysis of recent youth violence, student protests, or campus unrest in the United States has attributed much of its etiology to what is described as the wasteful loss of funds and people, foliage and food in Vietnam.

The United States waged the battle not supported, as we know, by the majority of the people, and even without rhetoric or tones of morality about that situation, I am asserting that the conflict can be described in the social psychological style of the laboratory experiment of auctioning a dollar—by promoting mounting frustration—which had an effect on youth. The youth were not privy to government information and were not participants in the decisions to escalate the conflict. Yet, nearly a decade of birth cohorts were pushed through the anxiety of military service in a cause in which they did not share. And so they saw the process as irrational and many refused to play, refused to invest the first 80¢ of their lives in a process that, from their point of view, was a zero sum game in which all is lost.

I think that, if one were to venture a prediction, in the future there will be less violence. I think that we will move into a period in which fraud and corruption and economic crime will be viewed as more serious, or certainly as serious as the crimes of violence that we saw escalating in the 1960s. I think that the changing age composition will have an effect on the reduction of violence. Simply the sheer numbers will be reduced for we have passed through a period of waves of youth who were the result of high fertility rates immediately after the Second World War and who therefore put a bulge in our population structure of those between 15 and 25, the age group most prone to violence. But as we continue to be more publicly conscious of fraud and corruption in high places and in business, we will begin to take more collective action against corporate crime. We may never get to the point where, as in the socialist states, economic crime, speculation, fraud, and corruption are viewed as larceny from the state and among the most serious crimes for which capital punishment still exists. But I suspect that we will move closer to that position in the future.

2

The Prediction of Violence

John Monahan

The desire to predict events in the world around us and thereby to gain some feeling of control over them may be intrinsic to the nature of man (Kelly 1955). Few events in life have greater physical and psychological impact than violence done to one human being by another. It is not surprising, therefore, that society would devote a great deal of resources to attempt identifying today the person who tomorrow will be violent.

In this chapter, I would like to explore (1) how society makes use of predictions of violence; (2) precisely what is meant by the term *violence*; (3) the empirical state of affairs of the accuracy of violence prediction; (4) several factors that might explain the dismal research findings; and (5) some social policy implications of violence prediction studies. Finally, I will propose an alternate and possibly more fruitful strategy for the prediction and prevention of violent acts.

The Uses of Violence Prediction

The task of locating the violence-prone rests primarily with the mental health and criminal justice systems. At least seventeen states include a prediction of dangerousness as part of their civil commitment criteria (Kittrie 1971), which results in approximately 50,000 persons each year involuntarily detained for society's protection and their own treatment (Rubin 1972). Of the 600,000 persons who will be apprehended and accused of index crimes against persons (homicide, aggravated assault, rape, and robbery) in a year, 5 to 10 percent will be given a mental health examination to advise the court about their potential for dangerous behavior, and an additional 10,000 persons will annually be confined as dangerous "mentally ill offenders," which includes "sexual psychopaths" and those found not guilty by reason of insanity (Rubin 1972). In addition, the judicial choice of probation or prison for "normal offenders" can be heavily swayed by formal or informal assessments of dangerousness, as can decisions about suitability for community rehabilitation programs or fitness for granting bail (Foote 1970; Dershowitz 1970). Predictions of violence likewise play a crucial role in deciding the transfer of a case from juvenile to adult court (Fox 1972).

15

While predictions of violence are often critical in deciding who will be detained for the protection of society, they are equally essential in deciding when that detention will end. The indeterminate sentence is perhaps the most extreme example of reliance on predictions of violence in determining length of incarceration. The individual is incarcerated for an unspecified or vaguely specified amount of time (e.g., 1 to 15 years) on the basis of his assumed dangerousness and released when authorities predict that he is no longer dangerous. Parole decisions in more determinate sentences also rely heavily upon predictions of violence (Wenk, Robison, and Smith 1972). In general, whenever a form of correctional or mental health treatment is applied to an assumed dangerous person, his release from the treatment institution (prison, civil mental hospital, or hospital for the criminally insane) is predicated on a negative prediction of dangerousness. The only way to know when the treatment of a dangerous person is over is to know when he is no longer dangerous.

The Model Sentencing Act of the National Council on Crime and Delinquency proposes that those found to be "dangerous offenders" could be given an extended term up to 30 years in prison. Yet the president of that organization recently called the identification of dangerous persons "the greatest unresolved problem the criminal justice system faces" (Rector 1973, p. 186).

Definitions of Dangerousness or Violence

An event must be delineated before it can be validly predicted. There is, however, no concensus among either legal or mental health professionals as to what constitutes a violent or dangerous act.

While Sarbin (1967) cogently distinguishes between violence and dangerousness ("Violence denotes action; danger denotes a relationship," p. 285), virtually all others hold the terms synonymous. Some define it to include only injury or death to persons (Rubin 1972), while others include the destruction of property. Violent *thoughts* are considered dangerous by some (Ervin and Lion 1969). In the District of Columbia, dangerousness is defined in terms of acts "which result in harm to others, or cause *trouble* or *inconvenience* to others" ("Comment" 1965). A federal court once ruled that writing a bad check was a sufficiently "dangerous" behavior to justify commitment (Overholser v. Russell 1960).

Goldstein and Katz (1960, p. 225) list the kinds of acts that might be considered dangerous:

1. Crime for which defense of insanity is invoked;
2. All crime;
3. Felonies;
4. Crime for which maximum sentence given;
5. Crimes categorized as violent;
6. Crimes that are harmful, physical or psychological;

7. Any conduct, harmful or threatening;
8. Conduct provoking retaliation;
9. Violence toward self;
10. Any combination of the above.

The Model Sentencing Act defines two types of dangerous offenders "(1) the offender who has committed a serious crime against a person and shows a behavior pattern of persistent assaultiveness based on serious mental disturbances and (2) the offender deeply involved in organized crime" (Board of Directors, NCCD 1973, p. 456). The Act comments that in no state would such offenders total more than one hundred at any given time. One may wonder, however, about the harmlessness of an offender who has committed a serious crime against a person and shows a behavior pattern of persistent assaultiveness *without* having a serious mental disturbance. Is society's legitimate need for protection any less in the case of crime by the socially deprived than by the psychologically depraved? Note that if one considers all repetitive violent offenders to have a serious mental disturbance, one has reduced the notion of mental disturbance to a meaningless and redundant tautology.

The working definition of violence adopted by the National Commission on the Causes and Prevention of Violence (1969) was "overtly threatened or overtly accomplished application of force which results in the injury or destruction of persons or property or reputation, or the illegal appropriation of property." Megargee (1969) notes that such a definition would include as violence accidental homicide, homicide in self-defense, injury on the football field, "or the newspaper reporter who exposes graft at the expense of someone's reputation" (p. 1038). He states that two issues confound the framing of a completely acceptable definition of violence. The first of these is legality. By ignoring legality and focusing on the act itself, the Commission has unwittingly characterized as violent various legal injuries to people. The alternative of defining violence in terms of illegal acts, however, "is to classify as non-violent the behavior of Nazi genocidists or Roman gladiators. . ." (p. 1039). The second nemesis of obtaining an acceptable definition of violence is the question of intentionality. The Commission's definition includes unintentional violence; yet specifying that violence can only be intentional or conscious would not hold well with those of psychoanalytic bent.

Review of the Empirical Literature on Violence Prediction

Despite the ubiquity of violence prediction in current mental health and criminal justice practice, there has been amazingly little empirical research on its validity. The studies that do exist, however, lead to very consistent conclusions.

Wenk, Robison, and Smith (1972) report three massive studies on the prediction of violence undertaken in the California Department of Corrections. The first study, begun in 1965, attempted to develop a "violence prediction scale" to aid in parole decision making. The predictor items employed included commitment offense, number of prior commitments, opiate use, and length of imprisonment. When validated against discovered acts of actual violence by parolees, the scale was able to identify a small class of offenders (less than 3 percent of the total) of whom 14 percent could be expected to be violent. The probability of violence for this class was nearly three times greater than that for parolees in general, only 5 percent of whom, by the same criteria, could be expected to be violent. However, 86 percent of those identified as potentially violent did not, in fact, commit a violent act while on parole.

The second study reported by Wenk et al. (1972) was undertaken in 1968 and was also in regard to parole decision making. On the basis of actual offender histories and psychiatric reports, 7,712 parolees were assigned to various categories keyed to their potential aggressiveness. One in five parolees was assigned to a "potentially aggressive" category, and the rest to a "less aggressive" category. During a one-year follow-up, however, the rate of crimes involving actual violence for the potentially aggressive group was only 3.1 per thousand (5/1,630), compared with 2.8 per thousand (17/6,082) among the less aggressive group. Thus, for every correct identification of a potentially aggressive individual, there were 326 incorrect ones.

The final study reported by Wenk et al. (1972) sampled 4,146 California Youth Authority wards. Attention was directed to the record of violence in the youth's past, and an extensive background investigation that was conducted included psychiatric diagnoses and a psychological test battery. Subjects were followed for 15 months after release, and data on 100 variables were analyzed retrospectively to see which items predicted a violent act of recidivism. The authors concluded that the parole decision maker who used a history of actual violence as his sole predictor of future violence would have 19 false positives in every 20 predictions, and yet "there is no other form of simple classification available thus far that would enable him to improve on this level of efficiency" (p. 399). Several multivariate regression equations were developed from the data, but none was even hypothetically capable of doing better than attaining an eight-to-one false positive to true positive ratio.

Kozol, Boucher, and Garofalo (1972) have recently reported a ten-year study involving 592 male offenders, most of whom had been convicted of violent sex crimes. At the Massachusetts Center for the Diagnosis and Treatment of Dangerous Persons, each offender was examined independently by at least two psychiatrists, two psychologists, and a social worker. These clinical examinations, along with a full psychological test battery and "a meticulous reconstruction of the life history elicited from multiple sources—the patient himself, his family, friends, neighbors, teachers, and employers, and court, correctional, and mental hospital records" (p. 383) formed the data base for their predictions.

Of the 592 patients admitted to their facility for diagnostic observation, 435 were released. Kozol et al. recommended the release of 386 as non-dangerous, and opposed the release of 49 as dangerous (with the court deciding otherwise). During a five-year follow-up period, 8 percent of those predicted not to be dangerous became recidivists by committing a serious assaultive act, and 34.7 percent of those predicted to be dangerous committed such an act.

While the assessment of dangerousness by Kozol and his colleagues appears to have some validity, the problem of false positives stands out. Sixty-five percent of the individuals identified as dangerous did not, in fact, commit a dangerous act. Despite the extensive examining, testing, and data gathering they undertook, Kozol et al. were wrong in 2 out of every 3 predictions of dangerousness (For an analysis of the methodological flaws of this study, see Monahan (1973c) and the rejoinder by Kozol, Boucher, and Garofalo [1973].)

In 1966, the U.S. Supreme Court held that Johnnie Baxstrom had been denied equal protection of the law by being detained beyond his maximum sentence in an institution for the criminally insane without the benefit of a new hearing to determine his current dangerousness (Baxstrom v. Herold 1966). The ruling resulted in the transfer of nearly 1,000 persons "reputed to be some of the most dangerous mental patients in the state [of New York]" (Steadman 1972) from hospitals for the criminally insane to civil mental hospitals. It also provided an excellent opportunity for naturalistic research on the validity of the psychiatric predictions of dangerousness upon which the extended detention was based.

There have been at least eight published follow-up reports on the Baxstrom patients, (Hunt and Wiley 1968; Steadman and Halfon 1971; Halfon, David, and Steadman 1972; Steadman and Keveles 1972; Steadman 1972 and 1973; Steadman and Cocozza 1973 and in press). All concur in the finding that the level of violence experienced in the civil mental hospitals was much less than had been feared, that the civil hospitals adapted well to the massive transfer of patients, and that the Baxstrom patients were being treated the same as the civil patients. The precautions that the civil hospitals had undertaken in anticipation of the supposedly dangerous patients—the setting up of secure wards and provision of judo training to the staff—were largely for naught (Rappeport 1973). Only 20 percent of the Baxstrom patients were assaultive to persons in the civil hospital or community at any time during a four-year follow-up of their transfer. Further, only 3 percent of Baxstrom patients were sufficiently dangerous to be returned to a hospital for the criminally insane during 4 years after the decision (Steadman and Halfon 1971). Steadman and Keveles (1972) followed 121 Baxstrom patients who had been released into the community (i.e., discharged from both the criminal and civil mental hospitals). During an average of two and a half years of freedom, only 9 of the 121 patients (8 percent) were convicted of a crime, and only *one* of those convictions was for a violent act.

One might also note in passing Megargee's (1970) extensive review of the use of psychological tests to predict violent behavior. He concludes, "Thus far no structured or projective test scale has been derived which, when used alone, will predict violence in the individual case in a satisfactory manner. Indeed, none has been developed which will adequately *post*dict, let alone *pre*dict, violent behavior" (p. 145). None of the testing literature of the past few years would modify his statement.

The conclusion to emerge most strikingly from these studies is the great degree to which violence is overpredicted (see Table 2-1). Of those predicted to be dangerous, between 65 percent and 99 percent are false positives—that is, people who will not, in fact, commit a dangerous act. Indeed, the literature has been consistent on this point ever since Pinel took the chains off the supposedly dangerous mental patients at La Bicetre in 1792, and the resulting lack of violence gave lie to the psychiatric predictions that had justified their restraint. Violence is vastly overpredicted whether simple behavioral indicators are used or sophisticated multivariate analyses are employed and whether psychological tests are administered or thorough psychiatric examinations are performed. It is also noteworthy that the population used by each of the research studies reviewed here was highly selective and biased toward positive results—primarily convicted offenders, "sexual psychopaths," and adjudicated delinquents. The fact that even in these groups, with higher base-rates for violence than the general population, violence cannot be validly predicted bodes very poorly for predicting violence among those who have not committed a criminal act.

We are left with the stark moral issue: how many false positives—how many innocent men and women—are we willing to sacrifice to protect ourselves from one violent individual? "What represents an acceptable trade-off between the values of public safety and individual liberty?" (Wenk et al. 1972, p. 401). No one insists that prediction be perfect. We do not, after all, require absolute certainty for convicting the guilty, only proof "beyond a reasonable doubt." That means that we are willing to tolerate the conviction of some innocent persons to assure the confinement of a much larger number of guilty criminals (Dershowitz 1970). But we insist on a process that minimizes erroneous confinement. How can this prized principle of our jurisprudence be squared with the fact that where the prediction of dangerousness is concerned, we are willing to lock-up many to save ourselves from a few?

Psychological Factors Involved in the Overprediction of Violence

To gain an adequate appreciation of the nature of the overprediction of violence, it may be worthwhile to speculate on the factors leading to this sorry situation. Attempts to improve the accuracy of prediction may benefit from an analysis of the processes underlying overprediction. The seven factors described below

Table 2-1
The Prediction of Violence

Study	% True Positives	% False Positives	N Predicted Violent	Follow-up
Wenk et al. (1972), Study 1	14.0	86.0	—	—
Wenk et al. (1972), Study 2	0.3	99.7	1,630	1 yr.
Wenk et al. (1972), Study 3	6.2	93.8	104	15 mo.
Steadman (1973)	20.0	80.0	967	4 yrs.
Kozol et al. (1972)	34.7	65.3	49	5 yrs.

Note: The definition of violence varies considerably across the studies. Wenk et al. (1972) define it as murder, manslaughter, assaults, rape, or kidnapping. Kozol et al. (1972) define it as "serious assaultive crimes." The 20 percent true positives reported for Steadman (1973) refer to those involved in "assaultive incidents." If the criteria for being considered violent are narrowed to conviction for a violent felony, Steadman's data show 1 percent true positives and 99 percent false positives.

might cumulatively account for the current state of the (in)validity of predictions of violence.

Lack of Corrective Feedback

The legal or mental health official who erroneously assesses violence seldom has a chance to learn of his error and modify his subsequent predictions accordingly. Those predicted to be violent are generally incarcerated on the basis of the prediction, and thus there is little opportunity to confirm or disconfirm the judgment (Dershowitz 1969 and 1970). It is not difficult to convince oneself that the predicted offender *would have been* violent had the state not preventitively detained him. A lack of violence after release is attributed to the success of "treatment," rather than to the lack of anything to be treated in the first place.

Differential Consequences to the Predictor

If one overpredicts violence, the result is that individuals are incarcerated needlessly. While this is an unfortunate and, indeed, unjust situation, it is not one likely to have significant public ramifications for the individual responsible for the overprediction. But consider the consequences for the predictor of violence should he err in the other direction of *under*prediction. The correctional official or mental health professional who predicts that a given individual will not commit a dangerous act is subject to severe unpleasantness should that act actually occur. Often he will be informed of its occurrence in the headlines ("Freed Mental Patient Murders Mother"), and he or his supervisors will spend many subsequent days fielding reporters' questions about his professional incompetence and his institution's laxity. "There may be no surer way for the forensic psychiatrist to lose power than to have a released mental patient charged with a serious crime in the district of a key legislator" (Steadman 1972). Given the drastically differential consequences of overprediction and underprediction for the individual responsible for making the judgment, it is not surprising that he should choose to "play it safe" and err on the conservative side.

Differential Consequences to the Subject

The prediction of dangerousness may often be nothing more than a convention to get someone to treatment. If the ticket to secure involuntary treatment is a diagnosis of dangerousness, many psychiatrists and psychologists appear willing to punch it. Once in treatment, the assessment of dangerousness is forgotten (Rubin 1972). To the extent that states tighten their criteria for involuntary civil commitment from "need for treatment" to "dangerous to others," one should expect predictions of dangerousness to increase. Overprediction, therefore, may be less a comment on any lack of scientific acumen and more a testimony to the ability of officials to subvert the intent of the law to accomplish what they think is "best" for the patient.

An alternate form of using the prediction of dangerousness as a ploy for other purposes is suggested by Morris and Hawkins' (1970) observation that when dangerousness is invoked, it often is for retributive purposes. There are some—for example, "mentally disordered sex offenders"—for whom the law requires "treatment" rather than "punishment" (Kittrie 1971). By diagnosing such persons as dangerous, however, one may satisfy tacit retributive demands by insuring that the treatment they receive will involve at least as much incarceration as punishment would have. Foote (1970, p. 8) puts it more strongly: he holds the concept of dangerousness to be "devoid of meaningful content and a convenient handle for political repression."

Illusory Correlation

An illusory correlation is a type of systematic error of observation in which observers report seeing relationships between classes of events where no relationship actually exists (Chapman and Chapman 1969). Sweetland (1972) has demonstrated how this phenomenon influences the assessment of dangerousness. Psychiatrists were surveyed to determine which personality characteristics they considered to be most characteristic of dangerous and non-dangerous persons. Following this, naive subjects were asked to examine personality descriptions that were made up of these characteristics and paired with the diagnoses "dangerous" or "non-dangerous." In one condition of this study, a zero correlation was present between the items designated by the psychiatrists as indicating a dangerous person and the diagnostic formulations with which these items were paired. Subjects were asked after the presentation to describe what they had observed. The results indicated that even when there was a zero correlation, the subjects responded as if they had observed a relationship in the materials. They consistently recalled that certain of the characteristics had appeared more frequently with the diagnosis of "dangerous," when, in fact, they were uncorrelated. These systematic errors of observation were consistent with the subjects' prior expectations about which characteristics implied dangerousness.

The poor ability of mental health professionals to predict dangerousness, therefore, can be partially explained by their reliance upon stereotypic prior expectations as to what constitutes a predictor of dangerousness, rather than valid correlations. Predictor variables that in fact bear no relationship to dangerousness will continue to be used because those who believe in them will find (illusory) support for their beliefs by selectively attending to the data: they will see only what they wish to see. The relationship between violence and mental illness, for example, is an illusory correlation (see below).

Unreliability of the Criterion

We have already noted the plethora of definitions that have been advanced for the designation of a violent act. In addition to the handicap of definitional vagary, research on the prediction of violence is actually research on the prediction of *discovered* and *reported* violence. Undetected violence and police discretion in certifying acts of violence necessarily decrease the reliability of the event being predicted. "The problem, then, is this: Most of the violent behavior we would wish to predict probably never comes to our attention, and the part that does is far from a representative sample" (Wenk et al. 1972, p. 401). A prediction of violence may itself be reactive—that is, it may influence the later certification of a violent act. Those at whom a finger has been pointed may be scrutinized more carefully than others, and the prophecy may thus fulfill itself.

Low Base Rates

A vexing statistical problem further complicates the prediction of violence. The problem has to do with the low base rates of violence in society—that is, an annual murder rate of 8.9 per 100,000 (Kelley 1973).

If the base rate of an event is high, predicting that event without many false positives is relatively easy. If 9 out of 10 people commit murder, one could simply predict that everyone will commit murder and be correct 90 percent of the time. As the base rate becomes lower, however, the problem of false positives becomes more salient. Livermore, Malmquist, and Meehl (1968, p. 84) address themselves to this problem in discussing dangerousness as a criteria for involuntary civil commitment:

Assume that one person out of a thousand will kill. Assume also that an exceptionally accurate test is created which differentiates with 95 percent effectiveness those who will kill from those who will not. If 100,000 people were tested, out of the 100 who would kill, 95 would be isolated. Unfortunately, out of the 99,000 who would not kill, 4,995 people would also be isolated as potential killers. In these circumstances, it is clear that we could not justify incarcerating all 5,090 people. If, in the criminal law, it is better that ten guilty men go free than that one innocent man suffer, how can we say in the civil commitment area that it is better that 54 harmless people be incarcerated lest one dangerous man be free?

Powerlessness of the Subject

Finally, the gross overprediction of violence may be so easily tolerated because those against whom predictive effort are mounted are generally powerless to resist. Prisoners or mental patients (who became or remained such due to overprediction) are unlikely to arouse a public outcry in their defense. As Geis and Monahan (in press) have recently put it:

The persons involved as patients-prisoners almost invariably are located in social positions where they do not have adequate political or financial resources to protest effectively against what is being done to them. That is, they lack things such as ready media access and funds to hire good lawyers. . . . If the aim is to isolate the violent, and to protect the innocent, then why are those who allow faulty fuel tanks to continue to be installed in the planes they market, and those who are or ought to be responsible for things such as an unconscionably high infant mortality rate (Gross 1967, p. 24) not similarly "diagnosed" and "rehabilitated."

Social Policy Implications of the Inability to Identify Dangerous Persons

The prediction of violence, of course, has importance only as an initial step in society's action in behalf of what it considers its own protection. Those predicted to be violent are involuntarily detained so as to prevent the occurrence of the feared act. The law normally requires conviction of a crime before subjecting a citizen to incarceration on the basis of a prediction of dangerousness. (Being denied bail on the grounds of alleged dangerousness is a form of preventive detention in which a crime has been charged, but not proven (Foote 1970; Dershowitz 1970).) The fact that dangerousness is greatly overpredicted would suggest grave caution in relying upon such predictions as a principle means for deciding who should be detained or when detention should end (e.g., indeterminate sentencing.) Given that past behavior tends to be the single best predictor of future behavior (Mischel 1968), one might generally weigh evidence of previous violence more heavily than clinical or judicial predictions (cf. Speiser 1970).

The one group in society, however, for which preventive detention is sanctioned, even in the absence of a conviction or allegation of a violent act, is that of the "mentally ill" (Dershowitz 1970; Monahan 1973a). This is no doubt due to the widespread public belief that the psychologically disturbed are intrinsically more violence-prone than the rest of society (Rabkin 1972). This belief is reinforced by the media, which frequently takes great pains to report that an offender is an ex-mental patient or has seen a private psychiatrist or psychologist, but never notes the lack of previous psychiatric history in cases when there is no such evidence.

The research literature on violence and psychological disorder, however, does not support public opinion. The most extensive review of the area (Gulevich and Bourne 1970, p. 323), which cited scores of studies, concluded that "an individual with a label of mental illness is quite capable of committing any act of violence known to man, but probably does not do so with any greater frequency than his neighbor in the general population" (see also Mulvihill and Tumin 1969, p. 444).

The lack of ability to predict dangerousness, combined with the similar base rates for violence among the psychologically disturbed and "normals," suggests that there is no empirical basis to support the preventive detention of those psychologically disturbed persons who have not committed a violent act (Monahan 1973d). A similar conclusion was reached by Pennsylvania's Task Force in Commitment Procedures (1972), which studied revisions of that state's mental health laws: "Since the capacity to predict dangerous conduct is no greater in the case of mentally ill persons than others, preventive detention is no more justified in the case of mental illness than elsewhere." Likewise, one cannot argue for the preventive detention of the mentally ill on the therapeutic grounds that they can be helped by psychiatric treatment, since no form of psychiatric treatment has ever been demonstrated to have an effect on reducing violent behavior (Monahan 1973b; Geis and Monahan, in press).

The overprediction of violence has even more sobering implications for attempts at prevention by the early identification of violence-prone children. President Nixon asked the Department of Health, Education, and Welfare to study the proposals of Arnold Hutschnecker, a psychiatric consultant to the National Commission on the Causes and Prevention of Violence. Hutschnecker suggested that psychological tests such as the Rorschach be administered to all six-year-olds in the United States to determine their potential for criminal behavior and that the tests be followed by "massive psychological and psychiatric treatment for those children found to be criminally inclined." Such a program, Hutchnecker said, was "a better short-term solution to the crime problem than urban reconstruction. Teenage boys later found to be persisting in incorrigible behavior would be remanded to camps. . ." (Maynard 1970). While some comfort may be taken in the fact that these proposals were resoundingly condemned by officials of all mental health disciplines, it is nonetheless disconcerting that they ever reached the level they did.

**A Proposed Strategy for Violence Prediction:
Identifying Violence-Prone Situations**

The conclusion suggested by the literature on the prediction of violence is that violence-prone individuals cannot be identified without erroneously identifying a much larger number of non-violent persons. The factors we have hypothesized to account for this state of affairs are not especially conducive to facile improvement. I do not wish to imply, however, that the task of predicting (and preventing) acts of violence is necessarily hopeless. At least part of our inability to predict violent acts may lie with the theoretical frameworks and research strategies that have constricted the psychological and psychiatric fields until very recently. Efforts to predict and modify violent behavior, like efforts to predict and modify all types of problems, have been almost exclusively focused on identifying *persons* who are likely to perform the behavior in the future (Mischel 1968 and 1973). It is becoming increasingly documented, however, that behavior is a joint function of personal characteristics and characteristics of the *environment* or *situation* with which a person immediately interacts (Mischel 1973; Moos 1973). The recognition that behavior is at least in part situationally determined opens an entirely new perspective on the prediction and prevention of violence. Rather than attempting to identify and modify violence-prone persons, energy could be expended in the attempt to identify and modify *situations* conducive to violence (cf. Wenk and Emrich 1972, p. 196). An ecological analysis (Moos and Insel 1973) shed light on the situational context in which violent crime occurs. Attempts to prevent violence could then take one of the following forms: (1) modification of the situation; (2) modification of one's response to the situation; and (3) avoidance of the situation.

In attempting to prevent the crime of violent rape, for example, a hypothetical ecological analysis of a given community might reveal that a sizeable proportion of past rapes occurred in certain areas of the community with poorly lit streets, at a time of day when women are walking home after bus service had stopped, and when women were hitch-hiking. Preventive efforts based on this analysis might then include modifying the environment by providing increased lighting and later bus service as well as a publicity campaign to advise women to avoid hitch-hiking situations (cf. the notion of "target hardening," Mulvihill and Tumin 1969, p. 776). Such preventive tactics are obviously not panaceas. Care would have to be taken not to induce community paranoia. There is always the possibility that would-be rapists will merely re-locate their activities in another environmental context. But to the extent that rape is situationally determined and "perceived opportunity" gives rise to sexual assault, such a strategy might have a significant impact.

As another example, a situational analysis of violence on policemen reveals that nationally 22 percent of the police killings and 40 percent of the police injuries occurred during interventions in family disputes (Bard 1971). Knowing, then, that family crisis situations are conducive to violence against the police, preventive efforts in the form of modifying police responses to these situations may prove fruitful. Training police to effectively deal with such violence-prone situations has already been mounted on a large scale (Bard 1971; Driscoll, Meyer, and Schanie 1973; Monahan, in press).

What I am suggesting is that social scientists divert at least a part of their energies from studying and predicting violent persons to studying and predicting violent situations. Such a change in tack might lead to appreciable gains in preventive efficiency (it could hardly do worse than current efforts at person identification), and would obviate the seemingly insurmountable problem of unjustly intervening in the lives of innumerable false positives.

Ultimately, it may be possible to classify both persons and environments in a typology of violence. One might then predict with some validity that a person of a given type will commit a violent act if he remains in one type of environment, yet will remain non-violent if placed into another situational context.

Conclusion

I have attempted an empirical and conceptual analysis of the prediction of violence and concluded that efforts to prophesy its perpetrators are doomed. I have also suggested an alternate strategy by which society might more effectively further its legitimate interests of self-preservation. Surely a citizen has as much right to remain unmurdered, unmugged, and unraped as he or she does to avoid unjust incarceration as a falsely positive case of dangerousness. The stark facts of current efforts to prevent violence, however, lead inexorably to the conclusions of Wenk and his colleagues (1972, p. 402):

Confidence in the ability to predict violence serves to legitimate intrusive types of social control. Our demonstration of the *futility* of such prediction should have consequences as great for the protection of individual liberty as a demonstration of the *utility* of violence prediction would have for the protection of society.

References

Bard, M. 1971. "The Role of Law Enforcement in the Helping System." *Community Mental Health Journal* 7:151-60.

Baxstrom v. Herold. 1966. *U.S. Reports* 383:107.

Board of Directors, National Council on Crime and Delinquency. 1973. "The Nondangerous Offender Should Not Be Imprisoned: A Policy Statement." *Crime and Delinquency* 19:449-56.

Chapman, L. and Chapman, J. 1969. "Illusory Correlations as an Obstacle to the Use of Valid Psychodiagnostic Signs." *Journal of Abnormal Psychology* 74:271-80.

"Comment, Liberty and Required Mental Health Treatment." 1963. *University of Pennsylvania Law Review* 114:1067-70.

Dershowitz, A. 1969. "Psychiatrists Power in Civil Commitment." *Psychology Today* 2:43-47.

———. 1970. "Imprisonment by Judicial Hunch: The Case against Pretrial Preventive Detention." *The Prison Journal* 50:12-22.

Driscoll, J., Meyer, R., and Schanie, C. 1973. "Training Police in Family Crisis Intervention." *Journal of Applied Behavioral Science* 9:62-68.

Ervin, F. and Lion, J. 1969. "Clinical Evaluation of the Violent Patient." In D. Mulvihill and M. Tumin, eds., *Crimes of Violence: A Staff Report Submitted to the National Commission on the Causes and Prevention of Violence.* Washington, D.C.: U.S. Government Printing Office, Vol. 13, pp. 1163-88.

Foote, C. 1970. "Preventive Detention—What Is the Issue?" *The Prison Journal* 50:3-11.

Fox, S. 1972. "Predictive Devices and the Reform of Juvenile Justice." In S. Glueck and E. Glueck, eds., *Identification of Predelinquents.* New York: Intercontinental Medical Book Corporation.

Geis, G. and Monahan, J. In press. "The Social Ecology of Violence." In T. Lickona, ed., *Man & Morality.* New York: Holt, Rinehart, & Winston.

Goldstein, J. and Katz, J. 1960. "Dangerousness and Mental Illness: Some Observations on the Decision to Release Persons Acquitted by Reason of Insanity." *Yale Law Journal* 70:225.

Gross, M. 1967. *The Doctors.* New York: Dell.

Gulevich, G. and Bourne, P. 1970. "Mental Illness and Violence." In D. Daniels, M. Gilula, and F. Ochberg, *Violence and the Struggle for Existence.* Boston: Little, Brown & Co.

Halfon, A., David, M., and Steadman, H. 1972. "The Baxstrom Women: A Four-Year Follow Up of Behavior Patterns." *The Psychiatric Quarterly* 45:1-10.

Hunt, R. and Wiley, E. 1968. "Operation Baxstrom After One Year." *American Journal of Psychiatry* 124:974-8.

Kelley, C. 1973. *Crime in the United States–1972.* Washington, D.C.: U.S. Government Printing Office.

Kelly, G. 1955. *The Psychology of Personal Constructs.* New York: Norton.

Kittrie, N. 1971. *The Right To Be Different.* Baltimore: Johns Hopkins University Press.

Kozol, H., Boucher, R., and Garofalo, R. 1972. "The Diagnosis and Treatment of Dangerousness." *Crime and Delinquency*, October: 371-92.

_____. 1973. "Dangerousness." *Crime and Delinquency* 19:554-5.

Livermore, J., Malmquist, C., and Meehl, P. 1968. "On the Justifications for Civil Commitment." *University of Pennsylvania Law Review* 117:75-96.

Maynard, R. 1970. "Doctor Would Test Children to Curb Crime." *Los Angeles Times*, April 5, Sect. A, p. 9.

Megargee, E. 1969. "The Psychology of Violence." In D. Mulvihill and M. Tumin, eds., *Crimes of Violence: A Staff Report Submitted to the National Commission on the Causes and Prevention of Violence.* Washington, D.C.: U.S. Government Printing Office, Vol. 13, pp. 1037-116.

_____. 1970. "The Prediction of Violence with Psychological Tests." In C. Spielberger, ed., *Current Topics in Clinical & Community Psychology.* New York: Academic Press.

Mischel, W. 1968. *Personality and Assessment.* New York: Wiley.

_____. 1973. "Toward a Cognitive Social Learning Reconceptualization of Personality." *Psychological Review* 80:252-83.

Monahan, J. 1973a. "The Psychiatrization of Criminal Behavior." *Hospital and Community Psychiatry* 24:105-7.

_____. 1973b. "Abolish the Insanity Defense?—Not Yet." *Rutgers Law Review* 26:719-41.

_____. 1973c. "Dangerous Offenders: A Critique of Kozol et al." *Crime and Delinquency* 19:418-20.

_____. 1973d. "Dangerousness and Civil Commitment." Testimony before the (California) Assembly Select Committee on Mentally Disordered Criminal Offenders, December 13.

_____. In press. *Community Mental Health and the Criminal Justice System.* New York: Pergamon Press.

Moos, R. 1973. "Conceptualizations of Human Environments." *American Psychologist* 28:652-65.

Moos, R. and Insel, P. 1973. *Issues in Social Ecology.* Palo Alto: National Press.

Morris, N. and Hawkins, G. 1970. *The Honest Politicians Guide to Crime Control.* Chicago: University of Chicago Press.

Mulvihill, D. and Tumin, M., eds. 1969. *Crimes of Violence: A Staff Report Submitted to the National Commission on the Causes and Prevention of Violence.* U.S. Government Printing Office.

Overholser, V. Russell. 1960. *Federal Reporter* 282:195. 2nd Edition.

Rabkin, J. 1972. "Opinions about Mental Illness: A Review of the Literature." *Psychological Bulletin* 78:153-71.

Rappeport, J. 1973. "A Response to Implications from the Baxstrom Experience." *Bulletin of the American Academy of Psychiatry and the Law* 1:197-8.

Rector, M. 1973. "Who Are the Dangerous?" *Bulletin of the American Academy of Psychiatry and the Law* 1:186-8.

Rubin, B. 1972. "Prediction of Dangerousness in Mentally Ill Criminals." *Archives of General Psychiatry* 27:397-407.

Sarbin, T. 1967. "The Dangerous Individual: An Outcome of Social Identity Transformations." *British Journal of Criminology*, July: 285-95.

Speiser, L. 1970. "Preventive Detention: The Position of the American Civil Liberties Union." *The Prison Journal* 50:49-52.

Steadman, H. 1972. "The Psychiatrist as a Conservative Agent of Social Control." *Social Problems* 20:263-71.

_____. 1973. "Implications from the Baxstrom Experience." *Bulletin of the American Academy of Psychiatry and the Law* 1:189-96.

Steadman, H., and Cocozza, J. 1973. "The Criminally Insane Patient: Who Gets Out?" *Social Psychiatry*, 8:230-8.

_____. In press. *Careers of the Criminally Insane.* Lexington, Mass.: Lexington Books.

Steadman, H. and Halfon, A. 1971. "The Baxstrom Patients: Backgrounds and Outcome." *Seminars in Psychiatry* 3:376-86.

Steadman, H. and Keveles, G. 1972. "The Community Adjustment and Criminal Activity of the Baxstrom Patients: 1966-1970." *American Journal of Psychiatry* 129:304-10.

Sweetland, J. 1972. " 'Illusory Correlation' and the Estimation of 'Dangerous' Behavior." Unpublished dissertation, Indiana University.

Task Force in Commitment Procedures, Commonwealth of Pennsylvania. 1972. Report. Pennsylvania Department of Public Welfare.

Wenk, E. and Emrich, R. 1972. "Assaultive Youth: An Exploratory Study of the Assaultive Experience and Assaultive Potential of California Youth Authority Wards." *Journal of Research in Crime & Delinquency* 9:171-96.

Wenk, E., Robison, J. and Smith, G. 1972. "Can Violence Be Predicted?" *Crime and Delinquency* 18:393-402.

3

A Multi-Dimensional Approach to Violence

Seymour L. Halleck

In spite of the enormous new interest in the problem of violence, progress in this field comes slowly. Neither the new impetus for research in violence nor the increase in publications and conferences on the subject of violence have yielded tangible gains. Rates of violence within the society have not diminished. A unified theory of violence still eludes us. Treatment programs for violent offenders are almost not existent. Preventative measures have been limited and unimaginative. All who work with violent people—including police officers, judges, sociologists, penologists, political scientists, and psychiatrists—share a sense of frustration.

There are several reasons for our lack of progress. First of all, each of our theories of violence has profound political implications. Different theories can be used to support different ideologies, and one suspects that at times the commitment to one theory or another is as much determined by the advocate's political beliefs as by his scientific expertise. If one insists that the roots of violence are embedded in the pathology of the violent individual, this assertion can be used to argue that our society is relatively blameless and that we could be spared the plague of violence if it were not for the irrational actions of a few deviant individuals. On the other hand, if one insists that violence is rooted in the basic oppressiveness of American society and that the variable of individual pathology is relatively unimportant, he is, knowingly or unknowingly, providing ammunition for those who wish to change our society radically. At the border of science and politics, it is extremely difficult to find objectivity. Deep emotions are stirred even by theoretical debate, and some of our conferences on violence have erupted in violence among the participants.

The passions engendered by ethical and political commitments are no less powerful when we turn to the issue of treatment or prevention of violent behavior. The ethical issues are excruciating. We have technologies that will change the behavior of potentially violent men, but the interventions we use often involve profound restrictions on an individual's liberties or have the potentiality of diminishing the violent person's physical or mental capacities. The political implications of prevention or treatment are just as complex. To the extent that any violent act is engendered by social oppression, that act can be viewed as a direct or indirect effort to bring about social change. If we somehow extinguish an individual's violent behavior without paying attention to its social causes, we negate the element of protest in the violent act, we distract society from considering the social causes of violence, and we support the status quo. Prevention of violence by working with "high-risk" groups has similar political implications. If we try to work with subcultures that have a high incidence of violence—such as black ghetto dwellers—we can be accused of defining the problem of violence as residing within the group rather than within the society as a whole. We can also be accused of using preventative techniques to smash the violent aspect of protest in the ghetto.

Finally, any type of intervention directed at preventing violence is limited by our inability to predict accurately the occurrence of a violent act. Even if our knowledge of the causes of violence were far more precise than it is today, there are so many factors involved in the occurrence of a rare event such as violence that prediction would remain extremely difficult if not impossible. Someday we may be able to quantify the probability of a given individual, living under certain circumstances, committing a violent act. But even if we can do this, the levels of probability are unlikely to be high enough to allow us to feel sanguine over the ethical and political results of interventions based on our predictions.

Given the above realities, it may well be that the most useful course those of us who work with violent people can take is to re-examine some basic questions regarding violent behavior. In this writer's opinion, there are three basic questions that must be considered by those who hope to understand, treat, or prevent violence:

1. How can we conceptualize the multiple factors involved in a violent act?
2. What type of social, psychological, and medical interventions are available for diminishing the probability that certain individuals will commit a violent act?
3. What ethical and political considerations should guide us in utilizing our interventions?

Conceptualizing the Causes of Violence

Human violence is a behavior that, like all human behavior, is determined by the interaction of the individual with his environment. A violent act is determined by who an individual is (his genetic make-up and his past learning experiences) and by where he is (the nature of the individual's total physical, interpersonal, and social environment). The individual environment interactional approach considers multiple factors as causes of violence but does not view these factors as exerting their influence in an additive manner. Rather, it directs the theoretician to consider the processes by which many factors interact with one another to eventually elicit a violent behavior. The approach can be illustrated by considering an abbreviated hypothetical example. Let us assume a young man is born with some form of dyslexia that limits his capacity to learn to read. Let us also assume that he is born poor and that his disturbance is not discovered by his parents, his school, or his doctor. During the early years of life, he finds that he cannot gain status and self-esteem by performing tasks that others do easily, and he is frequently shamed and humiliated by his teachers. During adolescence, he begins to find a certain degree of status and a means of venting his frustrations by associating with delinquent peers and engaging in occasional delinquent acts. He is sent to a reform school where he learns to protect himself and at the same time gain status by becoming physically aggressive. In the meantime, he is deprived of the kind of training that would enable him to find a role as a working, tax-paying citizen. In young adulthood, after having drifted around aimlessly for several years, he is drinking in a bar when another young man makes a statement that casts doubts upon his masculinity. Our subject at this point becomes violent and attacks his tormentor with his fists, and sensing that he is losing the fight, he pulls out his switchblade and stabs his adversary to death.

The above vignette describes a process of interaction of multiple factors that eventually results in a violent act. When viewing this process scientifically, we see that no single factor involved could be sufficient cause for our subject's behavior. Similar complex processes are involved in any violent act. Yet, anyone who reads the literature of violence is all too familiar with the tendency of professionals, as well as lay people, to blame violent behavior on single or monistic causes. Biologists emphasize inherited or acquired physical deficits. Psychoanalysts emphasize the impact of the subject's unfavorable learning experience with his parents. Educators blame the schools. Some sociologists are concerned with the subject's delinquent associations. Others talk about violent subcultures and the impact of poverty. Still other students of violence might emphasize the availability of technology, such as guns or knives, that makes it easy for people to kill in an impersonal fashion.

Thousands of hours are wasted, and splendid opportunities for interdisciplinary research are lost by seemingly endless arguments over whether biologic, psychological, or social factors are predominant in determining violence. Yet, it is obvious that no single factor or group of factors can explain an individual behavior. If it were theoretically possible to raise two people in identical environments, they would not learn similar patterns of behavior because they would have different genetic make-ups. Even if two people with identical genetic make-ups were raised in identical environments, their behavior would differ once each was exposed to a different environment. Finally, changes in the recent or present environment can never fully account for an individual's behavior. People exposed to the most oppressive environments react differently. Some tolerate oppression, others fight it, and others succumb to it by developing highly maladaptive behavioral patterns.

While the tendencies of scientists and laymen to ignore a process approach and to focus upon wholistic explanations is deplorable, it is also understandable.

Complex processes are not easy to study. Research requires that certain variables be isolated and examined in terms of their impact upon the individual's total behavior. Furthermore, examination of a process does not always suggest a logical rationale for intervention into that process. There is always some need for classification of the factors that go into a process and for conceptualizing how these factors can exert their influence and therefore be modified. It will be necessary then to briefly state how various classes of factors exert influence in determining violence, with the admonition to the reader that no single factor or group of factors can ever fully account for complex human behavior.

In order to facilitate understanding of how various interventions might diminish violent behavior, it will be useful to classify the causative factors of violent behavior into four categories: (1) biological, (2) educational, (3) environmental, and (4) informational.

If a violent act is to occur an individual must have the physical capacity to initiate that act. While there is much controversy as to whether man is biologically determined to be a violent animal, there can be no question that neurological and muscular mechanisms that can lead to violence are an inherent aspect of the human condition. In attempting to explain why some people are so much more violent than others, scientists have for decades sought to discover some biological defect in violent men that might increase their tendency to utilize the mechanisms of violence. Unfortunately, too many researchers who have felt that they have discovered such mechanisms have also assumed that they have discovered the cause of violence. Most of the all-encompassing Lombrosian theories, which seek to explain all criminal or violent behavior as related to some biological deficit, have been proven to be useless. More recent theories postulating that violence is related to some type of hypophalamic disorder (the six and fourteen syndrome) or some chromosomal anomoly (the XYY syndrome) have also failed to be substantiated by research.

Nevertheless, it would be naive to assume that no type of inherited or acquired biological factor could be influential in increasing the capacity of some individuals to utilize violent mechanisms. There is currently some highly controversial evidence that people who suffer certain specific brain lesions may be subject to periodic, epileptic-type behaviors that are characterized by violence. It is also true that people whose capacity to perceive the environment accurately are impaired by some type of general brain dysfunction (usually referred to as an acute or chronic brain syndrome) and may also be more susceptible to violent behavior than those who are not so impaired. In addition, there are many drugs, particularly alcohol and amphetamines, that so alter brain functioning as to increase propensity for violence. Finally, it should be noted that there may be a large number of people whose inherited learning difficulties have impaired their capacity to cope with the usual stresses of life and ultimately led to their learning behaviors that may increase the probability of violence.

Physical factors can also play a role in determining violence in an indirect manner. A tall muscular person may gain self-esteem easily through utilizing his strength in a violent manner. A short person may become gruff and aggressive to compensate for feelings of inferiority. An ugly or deformed person may seek out involuntary sexual partners because he cannot find willing partners.

Most of the psychological and sociological theories of violence emphasize the learning that those who become violent experience throughout early and adult life. Individuals raised in a climate of violence are more likely to be violent. So are individuals who are taught directly or indirectly to resolve conflicts through physical force. Those who grow up under situations of poverty and oppression and who have learned to distrust their fellow man are more susceptible to violence than those who grow up in more fortunate circumstances. It is possible that some people are taught to gain status and self-esteem through utilizing force. It is also likely that violent sex offenders learned to enjoy sexual activities with involuntary subjects. Theories of violence based on the individual's previous learning experiences can be highly complex, and the more sophisticated theories take into account how the individual interacts with his environment over a long period of time, so as to eventually learn violent responses.

Learning theories of violence also encompass the possibility that people are more prone to violence because they have failed to learn other need-gratifying and non-violent behaviors. The violence-prone person is often seen as one who has failed to learn how to gain esteem and status through non-violent means, who lacks coping skills, or who lacks the ability to express aggression in a sociably acceptable manner. Violent sex offenders are viewed as individuals who have failed to learn to relate to a mature member of the opposite sex.

Environmental factors in violence encompass all of the forces that impinge upon the violent person in the period shortly or immediately preceding the violent act. Stress created either by the violent person's family, friends, or co-workers or by the society as a whole can be an important factor in eliciting violence. Most murders and assaults involve people who know one another well and who are in conflict with one another. Usually the violent person and his victim are related to one another. Serious family conflict precedes many violent behaviors, particularly sex offenses. Stress emanating from larger social systems is a more subtle factor in creating violence. There is general agreement among behavioral scientists, however, that those who most powerfully feel the stress of social oppression are also most likely to be violent.

There are other factors in the immediate environment that may be necessary causes of a violent act. The availability and behavior of the victim is critical. There is a critical element of chance here. Many victims might have avoided being the subject of violence if they had altered their behavior in some critical way. The availability of lethal technology is also critical. If people fought only with their fist, it is likely that many violent acts would terminate once the loser had apologized or demonstrated some sign of his pain or suffering. When technology—which allows for assault and killing in a swift and impersonal manner—is available, the probability of severe violence increases. The environment may also encourage violence by reinforcing it. Where violence is romanticized in literature, in the press, and in films, it becomes more common. When it is taken for granted by the community or by the society as a whole, it is unlikely to be extinguished.

Informational factors are probably not as important as biological, educational, and environmental factors, but there are some interesting theories relating informational deficits to violence. From the time of Freud, psychiatrists and psychoanalysts have sought to prove that some individuals who are not aware of their own motivations may commit violent acts to resolve internal conflicts. A person may be aggressive towards others because he is unaware of his guilt, his depression, or his need to be loved. Lack of information as to how one influences others may also be a factor in violence. If a person does not know that he is angering or intimidating others, he may continue to act in a way that leads to an escalation of conflict and subsequent violent behavior. Finally, a lack of information about one's environment may be a factor in eliciting aggression and sometimes violence towards inappropriate objects. The person who does not know who is doing what to him is in a frustrating position. He may lack knowledge of oppression imposed upon him either by other individuals or by the society as a whole. Such a person may respond to frustration by violent activity usually directed against inappropriate objects.

Interventions to Prevent Violence

The above listing of factors that play a role in determining violent behavior can be taken as a starting position for conceptualizing the usefulness of interventions that might diminish violent behavior. It is necessary, again, to be clear as to what we are talking about when we consider changing violent behavior. The most we can do is influence the probability of a violent act occurring by changing those factors in the individual and his environment that are conducive to violence. Sometimes we deal with individuals who have already committed a violent act, and when we try to change factors conducive to further violence on the part of these individuals, we think of our interventions as treatment. We also interfere in the lives of people characterized as having varying degrees of probability of committing a violent act even though they have not previously been violent, and then, we are more likely to think of intervention as prevention. It should be clear, however, that in a broad sense, all of our interventions are preventative insofar as they are efforts to reduce the probability of the occurrence of a violent act.

There are five varieties of interventions currently available to help "treat" and prevent violence.

1. *Violent behavior directed at ordinary citizens can be prevented at least*

temporarily by putting violent individuals in drastically modified environments that so impair their mobility they cannot commit violent acts outside of that environment. When we imprison violent offenders, they cannot commit violence against citizens outside of the prison environment. When we use a form of preventive detention to restrain the mentally ill, they too cannot commit violence against ordinary citizens. There may, of course, be violence in the institutions to which these individuals are confined, but this too can be controlled by the degree of restraint imposed upon the inmate.

2. *An individual's biological state may be changed.* When a person is given psychoactive drugs, convulsive therapy, or is subjected to psychosurgery, his brain chemistry or physiology will be altered and his behavioral responses to environmental stimuli will be altered. Many of the biological interventions currently available can drastically change behavior and can be utilized in a manner that will reduce the probability of violent behavior. It is quite likely that in the near future we will develop even more powerful biological means of changing violent behavior. Obviously, biological therapies can either be voluntarily accepted by the individual, or they can be imposed upon him. They can in theory be used to change both those who have already been violent and those who have not.

3. *The individual's environment can be changed so as to provide him with new learning experiences that will diminish his propensity to violence.* In the new environment, behavior change is effected by reinforcing certain behaviors and extinguishing others. A new environment can be created either inside or outside of institutions; it can be either totally or partially different from the offender's old environment. Sometimes it is possible to devise total environments that reinforce "desirable" behavior and extinguish "undesirable" behavior. More often, behavioral scientists try to change behavior by setting up limited environments in which the client is either advised or directed to change some part of his daily life, or the client is given the opportunity to interact regularly with a therapist or counselor who provides a therapeutic climate of intimacy (or a new environment) in which new learning can take place. All of the conventional psychotherapies—individual, group, and family, to a certain extent—rely on the creation of a climate of trust and intimacy between therapist and client or between client and client, which allows for new learning to take place. Some of the newer behavior therapies do not require intimate interpersonal relationships as part of the field in which new learning takes place but require an impersonal and relatively precise structuring of the patient's environment.

Therapies that are based upon trust and close interpersonal relationships usually, but not always, require the client's consent. One of the interesting and ethically troubling aspects of the more precise behavior therapies is that they provide a rationale for creation of environments that can be imposed upon the client. A repressive environment such as a prison uses a crude form of behaviorism when it rewards certain behaviors and punishes others. But more sophisticated environments can be created by placing involuntary subjects into environments dominated by operant conditioning models, such as a token economy. This is a form of treatment in which the offender may have little choice in accepting or rejecting relatively effective behavioral change. The subject may not even be aware of how his environment has been deliberately orchestrated to bring about such change. (It should be noted that behavior modification techniques can also be utilized with the client's consent. The subject can be persuaded to cooperate in a series of treatment techniques in which he voluntarily enters a certain environment or tries to change his environment in a manner that provides for new learning.)

The learning experience provided within institutions such as the prison can be as powerful as those who run the prison are sophisticated enough and ruthless enough to make it. This is because the offender's captors have total control of the offender's environment. If there were no legal or ethical restraints upon prison administrators and if they employed the principles of behaviorism with sufficient technical skill, they should totally control the offender's behavior, at least while the offender is in prison and perhaps for a long time afterwards.

Those interventions that bring about behavioral change by creating new learning experiences within the environment can, in most instances, be used with both voluntary and involuntary subjects. They can also be utilized both with those who have committed violent acts and those who have not.

4. *Behavior can be changed not only by changing the contingencies of reinforcement within the environment but also by changing the nature of the environmental stimuli through an increase or reduction of stress.* Most maladaptive behavior is diminished when stress is diminished. Potentially violent individuals often change their behavior when they find even temporary relief from the stress of bigotry and poverty. They also change when the level of stress generated by their own families is moderated. The only conventional therapy that works directly at diminishing environmental stress is family therapy. But, it should be noted that any social intervention that reduces real social oppression in the person's life will also reduce the probability of his committing a violent act.

5. *Behavior can be changed, at least moderately, by providing people with new information.* The potentially violent person can gain new information about his own motivations (insight) and experience a change in the manner in which he perceives his environment. This change in perception may alter his responses to environmental stimuli. The offender can also gain new information or insight as to the impact he has on others. Such information will also change his motivations and perceptions. Finally, a potentially violent person can gain more information as to the nature of his environment. The manner in which such knowledge facilitates behavioral change has not been adequately conceptualized by behavioral scientists and needs some elaboration. A person who walks in the

woods and encounters a harmless snake will have different behaviors before and after the acquisition of knowledge that allows him to discriminate between poisonous and non-poisonous snakes. A person who is being treated badly by someone close to him but who does not know he is being treated badly may lash out at inappropriate targets. Once he perceives the source of oppression his behavior is likely to change. At a broader social level, we have seen that large groups of people, such as women and blacks, have changed much of their self-punitive behavior by acquiring greater knowledge or consciousness of the oppressions that society has imposed upon them.

All of the conventional psychotherapies—individual, group, and family—are in part designed to help the individual gain greater information about himself. Group therapies are particularly suitable for helping the client to understand his impact upon others. Family therapies often provide the client with new information as to how significant figures in his life are reacting towards him. In recent years, we have also seen the development of a series of consciousness-raising techniques in which behavioral change—often in the form of political activism—is facilitated by seeking to expand the awareness of oppressed people as to the sources of their misery.

Ethical Issues in Intervention

Having listed those classes of interventions that diminish the probability of violence, we can now consider the ethical and political implications of using each type of intervention. These implications can best be understood by considering the following questions:

1. To what extent is society justified in opposing restraints upon the freedom of those who have committed violent acts or are believed to be likely to commit violent acts?
2. How can we treat violent or potentially violent individuals whose actions may in whole or in part be determined by social injustices without becoming politically repressive?
3. Is treatment that diminishes the probability of violence justifiable, if the effects of such treatment are to reduce an individual's potentialities for future happiness and success?
4. Are we ever justified in imposing treatments upon a person against his will or without his knowledge?
5. Can we ever justify utilizing treatments based on depriving the subject of the basic human needs or amenities of daily life that are available to ordinary citizens?

The issue of using detention or incapacitation as an intervention in preventing violent behavior has received considerable attention in legal, criminological, and psychiatric literature. There is first of all the question of preventive detention of those who are not even charged with having committed a violent act but are suspected of being probable candidates for violence. Currently we do not detain such individuals unless we suspect that they are mentally ill. It should be noted, however, that involuntary commitment of mentally ill individuals who are believed to be dangerous to themselves or others is no longer taken for granted in American society. Many individuals now argue that the dangers done by depriving the so-called dangerous ·mentally ill of liberty may outweigh the advantages that involuntary confinement and treatment brings to either the individual or the society. Noting that psychiatrists have no special expertise in predicting violence, many states are now restricting the power of medical commitment except in instances where mental disorganization is blatant and the individual either makes strong threats of violence or has a history of violent behavior. In dealing with the problem of civil commitment of the mentally ill, society is obviously confronted with a complex choice. By opting for the value of liberty over the values of stability, health, or control, we may be risking a slight increase in the amount of violence some disturbed individuals direct against themselves or others. On the other hand, if we continue to commit large numbers of mentally disturbed individuals, it is probable that many will be unnecessarily deprived of liberty. My own feelings with regard to this ethical conflict are · that involuntary confinement of some emotionally disturbed individuals is justified if they have a treatable mental illness and if their threats of violence or previous violent behavior has been well documented.

Preventive detention of those charged with a violent act and not mentally ill is an equally complex issue. While our current laws guard against indiscriminate use of preventive detention, the courts can, by regulating the size of bail, keep some individuals under restraint. The current usages of bail seem, in principle, to be fair. The problem is that poor people are often unable to raise bail money. There are serious inequities in the manner in which potentially violent offenders are being restrained that will only be resolved by a sweeping reform of our bail system. The issues involved in such reform will not be discussed here.

The ethical problems in incapacitating individuals convicted of having committed a violent act are less complex, since our laws clearly call for varying degrees of confinement for such individuals. The problem here is determining the duration of that confinement. Should we confine violent offenders for a fixed period of time and risk the possibility of their committing a new violent act when they are released, or should we keep them confined until we have a strong conviction that they have been "cured"? The current trend in our society argues that the threats to the individual offender's liberty involved in indeterminate confinement or treatment outweigh the benefits of this practice. The skills of criminologists as well as psychiatrists in predicting subsequent acts of violence are so limited that people are now advocating that we do away with indeterminate confinement programs for violent offenders and return to the practice of fixed sentencing. My own views are that unless an offender is so mentally deranged as to qualify for commitment under civil codes, he should not be confined under a criminal code for any period of time longer than the customary sentencing for his particular crime. This does not mean, however, that indeterminacy cannot be used as a principle for releasing offenders from confinement before their sentences expire. If most violent offenders could receive adequate treatment while in confinement, they could safely return to society in a shorter period of time than that called for in our usual criminal codes.

Biological interventions can be powerful vectors in the prevention of violence. The society could, if it were ruthless enough, lobotomize those convicted or suspected of violent propensities. We could also massively tranquilize potentially violent individuals. We could addict people to drugs such as heroin and by controlling the supply of the addictive agent, thoroughly regulate an individual's behavior. Or we could implant electrodes in people's brains and control them by selectively stimulating their pleasure or pain centers. We could also diminish violent sex crimes by castrating sex offenders.

Obviously, such use of biological interventions has overwhelming ethical dangers. The dangers are most obvious when these interventions are suggested as treatment for involuntary subjects. But biological interventions raise troubling ethical questions even when they are voluntarily accepted by subjects. Sometimes the issue of voluntarism is clouded by threats of punishment. Subjects have accepted treatments, such as castration or lobotomy, with the knowledge that failure to do so would have resulted in prolonged incarceration. Even subjects who do not face coercive deprivation of liberty but who seek interventions to alleviate personal suffering may harm themselves by submitting to biological treatments. The highly tranquilized person does not function as effectively as the drug-free person, and drugs may mute his political motivations and activities.

One of the key issues in utilizing biological intervention with voluntary patients, whether the volunteer seeks them to avoid continued or imminent incapacitation or to alleviate personal suffering, is the subject's informed consent. It is hard to see how any of these treatments could be justified, on even a totally voluntary basis, unless the subject has been fully informed as to the potential dangers of treatment and the availability of alternative dispositions or treatments. If the patient is provided with such information in a scrupulous and detailed manner and still volunteers for biological treatment, the ethical issues are not all-consuming.

The considerable willingness of many subjects to use biological treatments at some of the so-called violence clinics suggests that the voluntary use of biological intervention will continue to play a major role in the prevention of violence. There is still the question of involuntary use of biological technology. Do we have the right to impose drugs, psychosurgery, or electronic monitoring upon subjects who have not sought such treatment? My own opinion is that in view of the possibilities of psychosurgery drastically impairing an individual's future capabilities, these treatments should not, given our current state of knowledge, be imposed upon subjects. The issue of drugs is somewhat different. If an individual meets the criteria of civil commitment I suggested earlier—that is, he is mentally ill, dangerous, and treatable—and if, in addition, he seems too deranged to be competent to make a rational decision as to the use of drugs, there is justification for imposing them upon him. In advocating these criteria, I am not distinguishing between those who have been convicted of crimes and those who have not. There are individuals who are appropriately described as mentally ill in both groups. Biological treatments should not be used to control behavior but rather to treat a suspected disorder that is causing the patient to suffer and may be at least one of the factors determining his violent behavior.

The possibilities of preventing violence through the creation of new environments is most promising. Individuals who have learned to develop behavioral responses that increase their propensity for violence can unlearn these responses and can also learn new behaviors that might diminish violent tendencies. Most of our current interventions in prisons, in hospitals, in out-reach programs, and in community clinics are based on re-educative efforts. Some emphasize individual psychotherapy, others group therapy, and others family therapy. Still others emphasize principles of behavior therapy. These programs are utilized with both voluntary and involuntary subjects.

The educational approach has far-reaching preventative implications. If we could discover what types of environments are most conducive to learning non-violent behavior and unlearning violent behavior, we might try to create these types of environments in our schools and communities. We might go even further and try to create a total society in which violent behavior was never reinforced and in which the individual from an early age learned non-violent responses. While I am personally convinced that violence could be significantly diminished by radical restructuring our social institutions, detailed speculation in this area is beyond the scope of this chapter.

It is hard to find too many objections to the use of interventions that provide new educational experiences by creating new environments when violent subjects accept these interventions voluntarily. Here again, however, the issue of informed consent has considerable importance. Most of the conventional psychotherapies and behavior therapies can be utilized in a political repressive manner. They may also have unanticipated behavioral consequences that the subject might not welcome. Any person who seeks some form of re-educative therapy, should be informed as to the potential negative effects of each of the traditional psychotherapies and behavior therapies.

The use of re-educative approaches with involuntary subjects raises more complicated questions. The conventional psychotherapies that require considerable cooperation from the subject cannot, of course, be imposed upon uncooperative subjects. When combined with the threat of deprivation of liberty, however, some individuals will gladly choose psychotherapy. Here, again, the justification for using these interventions with such subjects must be based on the individual's total awareness of all of the variables in his situation. The use of behavior therapies with involuntary subjects confined to institutions are more controversial since they can be employed without the subjects cooperation. Aversive therapies in which highly unpleasant chemical or electrical stimulation is paired with some behavior that the therapist wishes to extinguish has on occasion been utilized with involuntary subjects. I do not believe that this type of involuntary treatment is ever ethically justified. Some institutions have set up highly sophisticated, token economies or rewards systems for shaping conforming behavior. Too often these systems begin by depriving the subject of some basic amenity of everyday life and restoring it when he behaves. I do not believe that these systems should be imposed upon involuntary subjects unless they can be utilized without depriving the subject of basic needs and basic comforts. Even with this proviso, they should not be used unless subjects are fully informed as to what is being done to them, what principles underlie the treatment, and what possible consequences the subject might expect from the treatment.

Reduction of stress in the lives of potentially violent individuals could be a powerful means of reducing violent behavior. If the oppressiveness of bigotry and racism could be diminished, our society could be plagued by fewer violent acts. The limits of stress reduction are largely determined by the limits of political and economic change. Earlier it was noted that we could try to create a social system that minimized the learning of violent responses and maximized the learning of more peaceful behaviors. We could also strive to create a society in which oppressive stress was minimized.

Ignoring for purposes of brevity such global issues, we could at present strive to eliminate stress in the smaller social systems in which the potentially violent move, through interventions such as family therapy. By working with a subject's spouse, parents, children, friends, or employers, we can sometimes diminish the level of stress below a threshold that favors violent behavior. We could also diminish stress in the lives of potentially violent people by finding them jobs and providing them with specialized services that might compensate for their earlier deprivations. The troubling issues here are more political and economic than ethical. If we exerted special efforts to diminish stress in the lives of violent offenders or those suspected of being prone to violence, some might say that we would discriminate against those who are similarly oppressed, but non-violent, and that in such discrimination we might even be encouraging oppressed people to break the law.

It is difficult to determine the extent to which violence could be prevented by providing offenders with greater information about themselves and others. Certainly if use of the conventional psychotherapies were expanded as a form of re-educative intervention, many of them would be based on a concurrent effort to help the violent person find new awareness of his own motivations. There is much controversy in the behavioral sciences as to the extent to which insight facilitates behavioral change. The prevailing opinion is that it is neither a necessary nor sufficient condition of behavioral change but that it may in some certain circumstances be a powerful vector towards behavioral change. There is no reason to suspect that the impact of insight upon those who behave in a violent manner would be more or less powerful than upon those who are viewed as emotionally disturbed and are non-violent. The issue here is that we have never really made any sizable effort to use insight as a form of intervention in dealing with violent behavior. Whether such an expensive intervention is practical or even possible is, again, a difficult social decision. The economic issues involved in expanding the use of group and family therapies as a means of supplying the offender with new information are not nearly so perplexing. Group therapies are obviously more economical than individual therapies, and a powerful and useful new awareness of the environment can be provided by family therapy through a relatively brief intervention.

An increased use of consciousness-expanding techniques might increase the probability of behavioral change but would create new ethical issues. Currently, a number of violent men confined to prison have significantly changed their attitudes and behavior by developing a new awareness of how society has oppressed them. Black offenders in particular have gained a new sense of pride and identity that favors militant but often non-violent behavior. What would happen if instead of letting offenders develop a new consciousness of their situation through covert and anti-establishment organization, the correctional system itself would seek to help offenders consider the extent to which they have been victimized? It is possible to conceive of a correctional system that would help offenders learn about the social and political as well as the psychological causes of their violence. Such learning, combined with efforts to teach legal forms of social activism, such as community organization, might be a powerful tool for diminishing future violence. Undoubtedly, if the correctional system chose to "co-opt" the process of consciousness expansion now going on among offenders, it could direct the behavioral change derived from such processes in the direction of legal, rather than illegal, activism. But all of this has complex psychological and political pitfalls. It is questionable whether offenders would accept consciousness expansion from members of a social structure that is oppressing them. And it is questionable whether our society would be willing to utilize a form of therapeutic intervention that might eventually facilitate drastic changes in the society itself.

Conclusions

There are many interventions now available to us that, at least in theory, would help prevent a good many violent acts. The problem is that even if we try to prevent violence without changing the society, we are limited in our intervention by subtle political and ethical restraints. Whether considering the causes of violence or the prevention of violence, we must take a multi-dimensional or general systems view. We cannot do things to the potentially violent without considering them as individual and without considering the impact of our interventions upon society as a whole. There will never be simple solutions to the problems of violence. And any person who proposes solutions that ignore the multi-dimensional nature of the problem is more likely to escalate the problem than to help resolve it.

4 Reducing Violence in the Criminal Justice System

Hans Toch

The criminal justice system cannot afford to get stuck holding the violence bag; there are no resources in our ranks to deal with violence in the community. We are no experts at resolving degenerating marital problems, nor can we reassure the aggressively self-protective slum youth against the dangers posed by other aggressively self-protective slum youths. The best we can hope for is for a role in a consortium of institutions addressed to fundamental parameters of violence. As policemen, for example, we can refer jealous alcoholic husbands to a relevant social agency; ideally, we could even insure that they show up there. As detached workers, we can point gangs in constructive directions, productive of collective self-esteem—provided that someone furnishes the tools and facilities—and ultimately the jobs.

We must also not permit ourselves to hold the bag now thrust upon us of custodianship of the potentially violent. For one, the bag is too mixed. Those who have committed violent acts sometimes are violently recidivistic (or recidivistically violent) but often are not. Until foolproof classification systems become perfected (which is unlikely), attempts at long-term storage of those adjudged violence-prone raise substantial questions of ethics and civil rights. We are faced with legitimate anger inspired by nightmarish interventions proposed by interest groups of conceited professionals for the rehabilitation of violent men. Even listening to such proposals risks unfavorable mention in the writings of Jessica Mitford or adverse decisions in court. To be sure, we can use the old warehousing gambit. We can store the practitioner of violence until his adrenalin flow and his reflexes slow down. But running concentration camps for violent men is hardly the job of self-respecting professionals, and it creates climates that are not peaceful and non-violent.

This brings me to the juncture where we are of necessity left holding the bag—because it is our very own bag. This is the area of violence committed by criminal justice personnel or clients under our control. For instance, if a police officer shoots a fleeing burglar, or if he roughs up a suspect he finds obnoxious, he is obviously our business. If an inmate rapes another inmate, or if he knives a delinquent debtor, he is clearly our business. And if a member of the custodial force manhandles any of his charges, or if he overreacts to inmate harassment, he is unquestionably our problem. And we cannot afford to be sparing in time and effort to deal with such problems and to prevent their recurrence.

The usual measures taken to deal with violence within the criminal justice system have tended to be based on two assumptions that are mildly contradictory to each other. Sometimes we assume that violence is a product of individual personality, disposition, or pathology. We try to screen out or fire troublesome staff and to segregate violent inmates. I say "try," because we don't necessarily succeed; in the case of staff, there are unions and civil service rules. And inmates can be segregated just so far and so long.

We have also assumed that organizational characteristics can be modified to bring violence under control. We send out departmental orders about the exercise of force, and we expand community relations training; we classify and move inmates, so as to separate aggressors and victims; and we try to expand the scope of monitoring and direct supervision.

The reason why such strategies are limited is that they simplify the role of the variables they address and make no provision for the rest of the world.

To illustrate the first point, let me suggest what would happen if you screened out police officers who showed characteristics empirically associated with physical contacts on the street. According to our data (and those of other studies), you'd end up with, among other things, a patrol force of uniformly tall men, of at least two years of college, all of whom were married, and none of whom had served with other police departments. You'd also select men with the top scores in the recruit academy. I assume there are hundreds of other predictors that correlate with violent incidents, including the hypothetical sadistic tendencies addressed through psychiatric screening.

Aside from the issue of discrimination and the problem of manpower waste, you'd end up with a new type of police force with many emergent unknowns. One difference I can tell you about is that in terms of unrefined criteria of productivity, your new men will not conduct as much business as your current force. I'm not suggesting that violence is a function of productivity, because we know that it is not; but it is a function of a certain *type* of high productivity, which is not currently discouraged and, indeed, is often esteemed. And we don't have data to tell us what would happen to our predictors of violence if even your worst men operated in a setting that emphasized quality control in productivity. In other words, what the predictions predict is violence in a complex chain of effects that (like all chains) is heavily interdependent.

Similar points can be made with regard to individual predictors of violence. For instance, there are those who like to infer from police height statistics that law enforcement calls for physical resources that small men and most women cannot marshall. You might equally well argue that large men, being physically fit, would tend to solve their problems by fighting. But they don't fight—at least, not as much. What actually happens is that if physical impressiveness is heavily stressed, men at the bottom of the height range have more incentive than other men for demonstrating their impressiveness. And we have no test of what happens to shorter officers in a police setting that does not stress physical prowess because there is no such place. Any police chief who'd create such a setting knows that he is toying with risk of impeachment.

Taking the manipulation of organizational variables next, we find it notoriously ineffective. Where one can show impact, the success stories would hardly keep you awake. Thus I can show you that in Oakland a reform of the police academy (increasing the stress on community problems and role playing, decreasing the military atmosphere of the school, and so forth) produced a generation of officers who in *aggregate* had fewer incidents on the street during their first three months, compared with the products of other schools. On the other hand, this performance was far from randomly distributed among the graduates of either the old or the new academy. In both cases, *some* men were disproportionately violent. The effect also seemed to dissipate over time, so that clearly, other forces took over.

And in general, the problem with regard to organizational interventions is that they are subverted. First, those most involved in the problem tend to be least affected, because they are strongly and independently motivated; second, interventions tend to be drowned in ambiguity, ritualization, and resistances. No warden or police administrator I know assumes that if he issues an administrative bulletin, this document will be reverently read, understood in the terms he intended, and followed to the letter and spirit. The administrator knows that his edicts become one of many perceived (and resented) pressures around which his staff try to accomplish whatever they try to accomplish. As we examine the perversely independent notions of our rank and file, our attention is drawn to forces that are not rooted in individual motives or organizational pressures. What we discover is our own, home-grown version of the subculture of violence. We in fact discover that there are several subcultural layers and that each is promotive of violence. First, there are the rules that provide group sanctuary to violent men. These are the norms of never rat on a con or a fellow officer, or see that you tie your shoelaces when King Kong does his thing. They are the premises of solidarity uber alles, of unite (no matter what) because it's us against the rest of the world.

Then there are the norms promotive or prescriptive of violence in given types of situations. Some of these norms derive from the outside world, and some are role related. These are rules such as "you only give an order once," you teach lessons to wise guys, and you get respect by clobbering people who challenge you. There are also in-group norms, or sub-subcultures, such as the working assumptions of your stake-out or tactical units, your riot squads, and your extra-tough inmate power cliques. These norms are elitist and are built on advertised pugnaciousness. They are standards that tell you that your group is better than the peons becuase it is tougher and can prove it.

Norms such as these support each other in any act of violence. While Jack the Ripper and the Tier 5 Power Structure rape Hector Gomez in the shower room, the rest of the boys will chalk it up as a routine evening by the fireside, and the guards will tell you that the victim was weak and asked for it. Given the normative systems, it would be unthinkable for your uninvolved inmate to express disgust or to intervene. And it would be inconceivable for your guard to assert that a man deserves respect even if he fails to put up a suicidal struggle to preserve his manhood and honor.

But powerful as the subculture is, it does not *cause* violence. What it does is facilitate or enable violence to occur. Jack the Ripper does not spring full-blown from the prison yard, like the fruit fly in the pre-scientific jar. What Jack does is to avail himself of a favorable climate for his propensities. And prison walls do not a climate make—at least, not in the sense that rapes can be attributed to shower rooms or to limited surveillance.

Violence is a joint product—or a true interaction—of individual dispositions, of subcultures, and of organizational variables. Your violence-prone officer may join the police department relatively fearful and unsure of himself as a person. This fact does not make him violence prone. But supposing the following occurs: Officer Smith (who harbors fear and self-doubt) enters the recruit academy and is exposed to the folksy lectures of Sergeant Custer, assigned to Training while recovering from wounds incurred in what is known as "Custer's Last Stand." The sergeant is nominally concerned with "Patrol Procedures," but he regales his class with endless tales of daring escapades. He provides documented case studies featuring feats in which a quick draw or an unexpected charge netted the arrest of a dangerous man.

Sergeant Custer is followed in the syllabus by Officer James Atlas, discoursing on Safety Procedures. Atlas talks of the risks of policing, especially where elementary safety procedures (such as striking first, if in doubt) are ignored. Atlas avails himself as teaching aid of the department's long-term roster of fatal and near-fatal casualties in the line of duty.

While not in class, Smith spends time in the basement cafeteria, where current talk centers on an ambush or sniping involving a brother officer and the need for machine guns as protection. There are also discussions centering on assorted unsavory elements who are loose in the community at the time.

Smith leaves the academy for field training and is paired with officer Punchy Gonzalez, who has abandoned a career in boxing to become a policeman. During slack hours, Gonzalez regales Smith with memories of the "rough and ready" days of law enforcement in which worthy opponents were honorably subdued. He proceeds to demonstrate some of the principles involved—on two aggressively resistant alcoholics who seriously object to being arrested.

Three weeks after graduating from the recruit academy, Officer Smith has accumulated eight arrests for resisting arrest and two charges of assault on an officer (i.e., Smith). He also has been reported to Internal Affairs for allegedly unwarranted brutality. Investigation reveals a propensity by Smith to cut short verbal interchange by physically attacking his opponents. He claims that he sees himself faced with unpredictably assaultive suspects.

The person-centered approach to violence calls for the dismissal of Officer Smith. It ascribes Smith's precipitous reactions to emotional instability disqualifying a man for a career in law enforcement. Smith must be duly informed of his deficiencies and discharged. Unfortunately, this approach might founder on technicalities, since emotional instability is a very evanescent criterion. The charge could be violations of departmental orders, but these prove non-specific in their definition of what is necessary force. The ambiguity of the definition leaves Smith's reading of the facts as valid as the next man's (including his Chief's). Smith must be reinstated, carrying bitterness in his heart and harboring a sense of being arbitrarily harassed.

Organization-centered approaches to concerns such as those evoked by Smith can take several forms. There is the remedy of reforming the academy that would involve such steps as quality control of instruction. Aside from the usual difficulties (chronic scheduling problems and a paucity of help) it might prove worrisome that Atlas and Custer are highly regarded and popular instructors, widely praised as the most relevant members of the instructor pool.

The issuance of information bulletins relating to good police procedures could be another step. The impact of this move would be far from dramatic. There would be a pile-up of documents in line-up waste paper baskets, and some grumbling about the proliferation of reading material emanating from superfluous men sitting at desks.

And even if new personnel were to benefit from streamlined training and clear orders, Officer Smith would not. He would remain as a source of violent incidents, or as a surly, inactive, alienated man, manifesting discontent and communing with brother-officers of like-minded orientation. He would become a core member of a negativistic counterculture (and one of the more vociferous activists in the Police Benevolent Association).

What I am suggesting with this caricatured characterization is that anti-violence measures aimed at one segment of the violence-promoting sequence tend to bear the burden of neglecting the rest of the picture. Ideally, we must deal with the violence-prone person (hopefully reconstructively), reduce the violence-promoting characteristics of our organization and climate, and—most importantly—work with the subculture and its norms. The peer culture—to my mind— is the key juncture. Officer Smith may survive disciplining, and he may create violence even if he is assigned to the radio room or bicycle pool. But he is unlikely to survive adverse pressures and explicit disapproval from his peers. Even the Rapo Jacks of the prison yard—emerging smilingly from solitary confinement and defying supervision—would be hard put to carry on in the face of concerted rejection by their peers.

I am suggesting that the ideal violence-reducing program would be a conjoint attack on personal, organizational, and peer group forces sustaining violence; that the most potent fulcrum for intensive intervention is the peer group or subculture. What I mean here is not only that we ought to tackle the violence subculture in our ranks, but also that the subculture may be the place to start in attacking other things.

I have several reasons for emphasizing the peer culture. For one, the locker room is the source of resistances you get to other measures. It rejects person-centered approaches, because it assumes that these can set threatening precedents. It holds the premise that violence grows largely out of situational pressures, so that any group member is a potential candidate for transfer to Siberia. Even if the accusations are deemed meritorious (for instance, if the target is seen as a dangerous nut), there is always the concern with autonomy. If administrators can monkey with Smith (however unsavory Smith may be), they are more likely to later encroach on others.

The group resists organizational interventions because these circumscribe discretion, and because they imply that one's judgment may be fallible. Again, the merits of the case prove strangely irrelevant. In Oakland, there was intense grousing about a policy against shooting burglars. Those who groused loudest were men who insisted they would never themselves use guns. These officers confessed that there had been a pile-up of corpses in the streets. But they argued that priceless freedoms (such as deciding when to shoot) can fall prey to alien interference.

Interventions that survive resistance tend to be devisive. Those who administer them become suspected outgroup members, and they lose credibility and influence. Running a revised academy, operating internal affairs, or functioning as a disciplinary board are lonely assignments conducted in the face of disdain and relying on formal power to carry through. Information campaigns that "explain" interventions (as seen by administrators) are seen as transparent rationalizations of unsympathetic men out to castrate the ranks.

At minimum, anti-violence campaigns that work must make token efforts to involve the peer group in a participatory role. If one's prison has no resemblance to a therapeutic community, groups of inmates (such as inmate governing councils) can still be consulted on the curbing of forcible rapes. And even police chiefs who are not participatory managers can share concerns about violence with lineups of patrolmen.

In Oakland several years ago, we set a group of patrolmen to work on the violence problem.[a] These officers did research and made recommendations. They led groups of other patrolmen. The groups originated anti-violence programs. One of these was the Review Panel, which is a person-centered strategy. The review panel consists of police officers who know everything there is to know about the violence involvements of their colleagues. If an officer begins to make a habit of violence, a group is convoked to confer with the man and to help him. The aim here is never to come down hard and to criticize, but

---

[a]A book describing this project, *Agents of Change: A Study of Police Reform*, by Douglas Grant, Ray Galvin, and myself can be ordered from the Schenkman Publishing Company, 3 Mt. Auburn Place, Cambridge, Massachusetts 02138.

to promote inquiry and thought. If an officer discovers that he has a self-defeating pattern of conduct, he is encouraged to explore new and better options.

Most panel subjects have tried new approaches. We suspected this because they told us so. We know that they have when they stop producing silly incidents on the street. We have impressive statistics along that line.

There are a few who stray and persist in their depredations. With them, the panel brings in the brass (or the brass band). The subject finds himself facing peers *plus* superiors, *plus* representatives of criminal justice agencies. He gets asked pointed questions. It is made clear to him that no one—but *no one*—sees things his way. This approach (according to the statistics) is hard to resist.

Let me set the panel aside and address organizational reform, which is not (as the youth culture would put it) my bag. Our groups of police officers helped revamp the recruit academy. They planned and initiated a constructive field training officer program. They intervened in the radio room to reduce misinformation; they set up family crisis teams; and they helped create a landlord-tenant unit. Such organizational changes were aimed at violence, but had built-in aims other than violence reduction. A more human relations-oriented academy helps round out its graduates, and it reorients the force toward a service model. It may, parenthetically, reduce violence. What is critical from our point of view is that the administrators of the academy may be perfectly content and immensely proud, even if violence remained high in the department. Conversely, violence may be reduced, and experiments may fail. The radio room may become more helpful and may reduce negative contacts. By the same token, it may develop low morale and staff conflicts or it may neglect key functions. It seems hard to insure that violence reduction remain alive as a goal. By the same token, if other interests are not protected, programs drag their feet. I am speaking here as a penitent man who has stood justly accused of wanting the tail of violence to wag the dog of policing.

My other point about organizational change is that it becomes smug. The custodians of new interventions are vested interests, and they defend and protect their turf. Our violence groups were innovative because they studied a problem and headed *toward* a solution. Those administering the solutions often felt that whatever they did must be responsive and appropriate. They had lost the humble problem-oriented focus. They had also sometimes lost sight of their goals. The field training coordinator was not bothered when he discovered that his training officers were strong, loyal, but unsympathetic to human relations concerns. And our family crisis teams charged ahead, without a self-questioning or self-critical bone in their body. It took us months to secure the admission that their perfection could (just possibly) stand improvement.

I mention these facts because I think they pertain to our subject more than to others. First, we must recall that criminal justice agencies are not by preference crusaders against violence; violence is a tool they use. This means that even if the designers of an intervention are concerned with violence reduction, those down the assembly line are likely to give this aim a much lower priority. Second, anti-violence campaigners know that their locker-room-mates do not hate violence. They therefore feel constrained to "sell" their role on grounds other than violence-fighting. Ultimately they often sell themselves on their own sales pitch. There is also the fact that you expect promotion efforts to reduce program quality, because experimental programs must be sold as products, with no loose strings or open questions.

The influence of the peer culture strikes me as a continuing enemy in campaigns against violence. Even in our own "honeymoon" days, with the anti-violence forces solid behind us, the pull of the locker room was ever-present in our midst. It encircled us, seduced us, cast shame and doubt among us. It met us in the coffee shop in the shape of jokes or questions. It met us in the street with snide, unfair comments. It entered our meetings with interviewees who regaled us with their blood and thunder tales.

We tried to create a subculture of our own, a subculture immunized—with data and thought—against the dogmas of others. We tried to build strength through performance, to remove self-doubt, and to feed potency. And we provided status, resources, and backing. Yet, the battle went on, and at times went badly. For no one can be insulated against the loneliness that is the fate of the rejector of norms. And no one can erase the nostalgic impact of past views. I am reminded of an ex-inmate who just recently gave me a paper on violence in prison. This man deplored the facts he reviewed; he urged an end to the slaughter in the yard. But in the end, he told me that to maintain one's integrity (and to stave off attack) an inmate must strike first, and strike well.

Our program in Oakland worked despite its in-built problems. Some reasons for its success are probably unique. They may be hard to replicate elsewhere. They involve the sustained character of our effort—the fact that we met for eight-hour periods two days a week, week in and week out. We also had a superb chief, healthy NIMH support, and some of the best officers in the country. And we had a great staff. Doug Grant is an innovator in the self-study area; he is also a veteran of training ventures involving inmates and para-professionals. Ray Galvin is a police expert who knows everything about the police business. In addition, he is a good trouble-shooter and arranger of details.

But then, we also labored under what must seem like real handicaps. Most of our men were hard-core violence-prone officers. We selected them this way because we aimed at the heart of the locker room. We wanted (in the words of Doug Grant) to use the problem as a means to solve the problem. And it is a fact that several of the most troublesome members of the Oakland Police Department are now travelling to other departments to help them deal with violence in their midst. Others are active in Oakland, running programs, and staffing them.

But we did not always succeed. Particularly in the early months some of our graduates were knocking heads and closing patrol car doors on people's arms and legs. One of our men resigned to continue the full-time real estate business he had been running (full-time) while on the force. Others are undistinguished and will stay that way. In the long run, however, we have done surprisingly well, and our alumni are doing their work largely without force.

I think part of the reason for our success is generic. For one, subcultural influence must be a two-way street. While the locker-room is seductive, the new subculture has its own attractions. It is prestigious and self-consciously sophisticated. It offers the man in trouble (under pressure by management) a way out. And there is the role of what (in the absence of a better word) we call "science." Violence problems are subject to review, with data on hand. Myth, folklore, untested faith are compared, for the first time, with facts. Most any man (whether guard, inmate, or police) is partly, at least, a rational man. At minimum, he will respect data he has collected.

Lastly, there is the role. Most persons in the criminal justice system tend to go about with little thought and communication about their roles. They do their time; they bury their basic doubts and questions under a cloak of false surety. They also suppress their fears and frustrations or take them out on management. The system is permeated with the myth of the "manly man" who doesn't have feelings, even when close to despair. There must be something seductive and important about a climate in which basic questions can be explored in the company of others sharing one's fate. And there is the feel of impact on one's own acts and one's setting. Particularly for the violent, who are alienated, it seems strange to test the premise that one is helpless in the face of alien pressures. In the role of innovator, a man discovers to his delight that he can be the source of what happens in his organization, in his work, and in his life.

This element is crucial in the work of our review panels. Panel subjects and panel members (we use our subjects as members of subsequent panels) see themselves as participants in the process. The subject must think through his own problem, with data about himself provided through his own arrest reports and his answers to questions. The officer serves as the expert on himself, and as a man who can determine the way he exercises discretion. He arrives at his solution with the approval and support of peers. And the panelist acts as a clinical analyst, as a change agent, and as an expert on police work. He reviews records in search of patterns. He works on the problem of approaching subjects to make them comfortable and amenable. And he provides the benefit of his views where appropriate. The panelist becomes linked to his own organization, because he sees police activities as they relate to violence patterns. He is thus a professional, somewhat like a physician at a staff meeting or a lawyer at a team conference.

Let me hasten to state that beyond the panel procedure, I do not perceive the Oakland effort as something to be emulated. I am not ashamed of our work, but I think of interventions as growing out of their own settings. I think the peer subculture must have a stake in its program and that such a stake can only emerge out of participation in program design. Beyond this dictum, I have a few rules to suggest.

1. I think life experiences, or job experiences, are the place to begin one's work. If inmates are to understand and counter violent rapes, or if guards are to deal with force used by guards, they must start by reviewing actual situations at issue. They must separate the givens from the options, derive a feeling for pressures, motives, and antecedents. They must rely on their own personal observations and pool these to make them reliable. They can supplement their first-hand knowledge with data as they feel a need for it. Here, dramatic information (such as interviews) have advantages over statistics. You may know of programs in the police field in which officers make lists of variables for computer analysis. I do not sense that the officers in these programs are relating their research to police experience. They seem to have no feel for the problems they study, because there is no relevant source of insights.

2. There must be informed backing from the organization. Support from the top is crucial, at first. It provides security that compensates for separation from the peer group. It joins the innovation (as the men perceive it) with aims of the organization. By the same token, sharing with other segments of the organization (and especially with peers) allays anxiety and provides a sense of mission. It also gives others an opportunity to buy into the program if they wish to do so.

3. A continued target focus seems essential. Any group is apt to see itself as a forum for ventilating grievances and as a vehicle for general reform. At the risk of creating discomfort, we must remind groups (sometimes forcefully) of their task. We must also maintain them product-oriented, which is sometimes hard. Programs must be worked out rather than being left as vague prescriptions. And "information campaigns" (spreading the word among the unwashed) must be avoided, as a tempting substitute for action. This is particularly true because a rationalistic view of change is often a disguised way of gaining goodwill or of leaving the hard work to others.

4. There must be contagion within the peer culture. This means starting out with strong figures who are widely respected. It means that there must be a search for links into the peer group, in which influence spreads outward. The inmate group working on inmate problems must not be permitted either to be seen as a "fink group" or to be used as a vehicle for peer grievances. It must enlist support on its own terms, by organizing study groups in the tiers, through problem-centered task forces, or by enlisting persons as visiting experts or temporary members. Continued contact of any kind with influence sources is essential.

5. Ultimately, the group must involve problem people. Different settings can promote special ways of handling this step. One way to manage it is to try to do it from the start, by mixing violent men with a group of strong positive members; or one can try peer interviews protected by assured anonimity. Or one can seek self-defined converts intent on spreading the benefit of their newfound

convictions. Whatever the gambit, the aim must be to bridge to the target group before it experiences the intervention as more pressure from an organization out to get it.

In summary, I have suggested that (whether we like it or not) violence in criminal justice is not the product of odd, sadistic, and malevolent men. Officers who punish and inmates who terrorize other inmates are in part responding to their settings—to our settings. They are not responding as we wish them to, and they are distorting our message, but they see themselves as obedient to our mandates and as responsive to our pressures.

We cannot assure the inmate that he is *not* engulfed by a power-centered jungle, nor can we tell the officer that life on the beat is free of danger and of challenges to his manhood. For the fact is that the parameters of the system (and the actions of people beyond our control) carry the contrary message for us. In prison, we have sequestered, collectively, large numbers of frustrated men. We have placed in charge of them other men whom we have instructed to control or manage. And we send men into the street telling them to subdue dangerous villains waiting to assail them around the next corner.

The emphasis in the system—even more than in our society at large—is on the exercise of violence as a means to solve problems. If we talk of positive interpersonal relations, we do so as an afterthought or footnote. Worse still, we send double messages. We order our officers to go out and control, and we become concerned if some take us more literally than others. We define men as custodians, and we complain if they arise, with alacrity, to the task. As for our inmates, we warn them about the danger of their fellows. We object, of course, if inmates turn tables on others with the viciousness of fear.

Ultimately, I suspect, we can hope for no solution that does not involve reordering our priorities. We can expect non-violent guards when we recognize that the guard is first and foremost an arbiter, counselor—a source of help to the stressed. And we can expect non-violent officers when we tell the police that we see them as a front line source of human service.

And we must be ready (if we are serious about violence) to give our clients positive roles within their institution and their peer group. We must help inmates with evolving their communities, collectivities in which the strong help the weak and in which cooperation brings solutions to life problems.

And we must join together—staff and clients alike—to address a fate and a challenge we all ultimately share.

5

Victims of Crimes of Violence and the Criminal Justice System

Gilbert Geis

Two fundamental conditions, seemingly operating at cross-purposes, bear upon the victim of criminal violence when he comes to define his response to his situation and his attitude toward the person who victimized him. On the one hand, he generally desires revenge. On the other hand, he often wishes to establish an appearance of mercifulness, to seem to possess an educated understanding of the imperatives that drove the offender to act as he did. A particularly useful catalyst for reconciling these rather contradictory feelings lies in the concept of offender "sickness,"–that is, in the setting forth of the view that there is something mentally wrong with the murderer, rapist, or mugger, and that such aberration merits compassion–or, at the least, mediation of any desire for direct retaliation. Since the offender is "sick," however, and since cure is taken as unlikely, by far the most sensible policy, the victim often suggests, would be to eliminate the offender or at least to isolate him for a very long period of "treatment." Advocacy of such a position allows the unification of what might at first have seemed to be irreconcilable impulses for vengeance and for understanding. Revenge may be had without guilt, and compassion may be indulged without compromising retributive feelings.

Numerous illustrations of such thought patterns turned up in interviews that colleagues and I conducted among victims of violent crime in California who had applied for public compensation funds. "He seemed to expect me to talk to him in the courtroom," one of the victims noted. "He looked kinda like a crazy man." A woman, who was requested to describe her assailant, called him a "sex maniac." Another victim, asked for an opinion about what she believed ought to be done to the man who had raped and savaged her, noted:

Just give him to me. I shouldn't feel this way, but I could kill him. If he did this to me, he could do it to others. He's really sick. If he can be helped, he should be. But if he can't be helped, why waste taxes on him? He should not be in society.

Similar kinds of responses—rather than those concentrating on socioeconomic factors or situational imperatives in the offender's background—were put forward in about two out of three instances, though occasionally there were refreshing variations, such as the victim of a pursesnatch assault who looked puzzled when we asked her what she thought was the cause of the offender's

61

behavior. "How should I know?" she asked in return. "I didn't stand there and talk with him." Equally idiosyncratic was the good-natured victim who had only sympathy for an assailant who had severely battered him during a barroom brawl. Perhaps, in this case, the important condition was the rather blithe attitude the victim himself had toward law violation. Asked if he had ever been arrested, he said: "Only once and that really wasn't nothing. They got me for 'disapposure' in an alley downtown. The cops just got right there before I had a chance to put it back in my pants." He smiled sheepishly and ended: "But I never was so slow again . . . they never had to arrest me no more."[1]

The nature of responses of victims of criminal violence and the form in which such response are related to elements of the criminal justice system constitute the subject matter of this chapter. Material will be drawn from the California victim compensation applicant interviews and from more recent interviews with survivors of homicide victims. This material will be supplemented with insights offered in the still-rather-sparse published literature on crime victims.[2]

It must be particularly appreciated that the crime victim rarely is able to see himself as an entirely guiltless person, an individual who has no necessity to review his actions and attitudes in order to understand what happened to him.[3] If nothing else, he must satisfactorily resolve questions relating to the lottery of human existence that resulted in injury being visited upon him rather than another. He must have at least some anodynic answer to the question of "Why me?" or thereafter must become fixed in the discomforting position that existence is hopelessly haphazard and that there is little gain to be had from rational, self-protective, planned action.

Too many alternative ways of behaving usually had been available to the crime victim (unlike, say, the cancer victim) to allow much ready surcease from soul-searching; a better door lock, more care in choosing the route to one's destination, availability of a gun or other weapon, more awareness of the danger from certain kinds of persons—these and a host of other "but ifs" nag at the victim. Almost inevitably, then, some blame attaches to one's self. Partial relief from unnerving self-doubt can be had by recourse to particular attitudes toward elements of the criminal justice system and toward the offender. We have no sophisticated data yet on the precise ingredients of such attitude linkages, but we can provide some details and offer possible interpretations of the form they often take.

Plight of the Crime Victim

Interviews indicate that no segment of the criminal justice system is altogether spared the anger and disdain of crime victims. Many victims feel that their needs have low priority in the business of the police, the courts, and the correctional system. They feel that they are, at best, tolerated and then often only with ill-humor. Their role, they say, seems much like that of the expectant father in the hospital at delivery time; necessary for things to have gotten underway in the past, but at the moment rather superfluous and mildly bothersome. Victims will sometimes note that the offenders seem to fare a good deal better than they do; the offender, at least, is regarded by criminal justice functionaries as a doer, an antagonist, someone to be wary of, a person who must be manipulated successfully if the workers in the criminal justice system—the police, the judge, the attorneys—are to have their satisfaction and rewards for a job well done.

The victim, on the other hand, is part of the background scenery—a rather drab character, in the nature of a spear-carrying supernumerary, watching from a distance the preening and posturing of the prima donna stars in the drama. There have been, on occasion, frank acknowledgements of this condition by members of the criminal justice establishment. "Railroads for some time have not done much to pleasure the customer," a defense attorney has noted. "Our system has been behaving like a railroad, because maybe it figures the victim can't just choose another court system. We've got to look at the victim like he's a customer who requires service."[4]

More often, however, even these kinds of expression of concern with the plight of crime victims are lacking, so insignificant do victims appear to those engaged in the process of dealing with the criminal offender. In this regard, the President's Commission on Law Enforcement and Administration of Justice noted that "one of the most neglected subjects in the study of crime is its victims: the persons, households, and businesses that bear the brunt of crime in the United States."[5] A law professor has echoed this observation. "Surely there will be agreement," Childres writes, "that some attention should be diverted from the criminal, one of the most vigorously studied animals in history, to his victim, one of the most ignored."[6]

One of the few outlets available to crime victims for expression of their concerns are the letters-to-the-editor columns of metropolitan newspapers. Some of the feelings that victims have can be gathered from a sampling of letters that appeared in *The New York Times* during 1971. It should be noted that many of the letters reproduced are from persons suffering property losses; presumably, victims of violent crimes would feel even more aggrieved.

First, there is the disillusionment with the bail system, shock at the apathy of those charged with apprehending an offender who fails to appear in court, and disgust with the role of appointed counsel for the defendant in thwarting what are seen as fundamental principles of justice:

On October 19, I encountered a thief who had broken into my parked car and who was in the process of removing the FM radio tuner. I followed him for eight blocks and was fortunate enough to spot a police prowl car. The man was duly arrested and charged. In his possession was the FM tuner.

That evening, playing the role of "good citizen," I spent three hours in night court waiting my chance to see justice administered. Taken before Judge Hyman

Skolniker, the defendant pleaded "not guilty." . . . Because of a legal complication, the prisoner, to my great shock, was released without bail despite the fact that he admitted to being a heroin addict with a previous arrest record. . . . The entire court appearance lasted between sixty and ninety seconds.

On October 28, the defendant failed to appear in court. As one who took the trouble to follow, to apprehend, and to appear in court, I am totally disillusioned with the results. I am informed by the Appearance Control Project people at the District Attorney's office that no one will attempt to locate the defendant. I was told that his failure to appear in court will merely be recorded and that should he ever be re-arrested, he will then face the music.

Basically what has happened is that this man has been given license to commit more crimes. This has been effected by sixty-second justice administered with the help of Legal Aid Society lawyers.

From my point of view, I deeply regret being involved and having wasted my time in the interest of justice. Should this situation recur (and I have no doubt that it will), I will not participate. Should I witness a crime, I will turn my back. It is obvious that under our present court system the victim gets no redress, and the petty criminal, when caught, goes free.[7]

A second writer complains that he met with "bureaucratic obstructionism" when he tried to obtain a weapon with which to protect himself against crime, while offenders readily obtain guns through extralegal channels, he claims. This person adds a lament against what he believes to be the press' insensitivity to crime victims:

. . . It is the law-abiding citizen who is most often the victim and it is for them that no protection exists under law. While the criminals' rights are zealously guarded by ever-watchful libertarians, the victims writhe in suffering and pain, suffer permanent harm and disfigurement or death, and great newspapers talk of the rule of law.[8]

I do not advocate unlimited access to guns or to weapons of any type, but until the law of the jungle is repealed in this city and across America, surely, who can criticize the man able and willing to defend his life through use of a legally registered weapon.

Further, as the witness who can identify the assassins who attacked him, the press places the victim once again in jeopardy of his life by publishing his home address, tempting the killers to murder him or members of his family in their home. Again we see that there is no protection under law for the victim but only the law of the jungle.[9]

Another writer contrasts the care and concern afforded the offender when he is incarcerated in contrast to the neglect of the crime victim:

Your July 26 news story about the Rikers Island Reformatory again reveals the city administration's perversion of justice and retribution. The story deals extensively with . . . the alleged denial of adequate training and rehabilitation to youthful offenders, and their subjection to "empty days and useless work."

But what of their victims? Are their days, in many cases, not tragically empty? . . . When will the Legal Aid Society, the city's public defender organization, bring suit to require that our elected officials protect the victims and not the muggers, murderers, the rapists, the thieves?

It would seem proper to assume that the offenders are in jail not because of virtuous behavior but rather because of explicit and, at times, recidivistic acts of violence, acts that cannot be tolerated. More sympathetic attention must be paid to the victims (whose numbers grow daily) and less cajolery—or none—given to the criminal element.[10]

A businessman, owner of eleven stores in Manhattan, reports that they had been broken into on 49 occasions during a two-year period. Every store had been victimized at least once. Finally, an arrest was made. The owner details the events that followed:

Our friendly neighborhood burglar . . . broke the locks in three [display] windows—looting the contents. When the fourth window resisted his best efforts, he broke the glass. A nearby guard phoned the police, who found a 41-year-old man up to his armpits in shirts and ties. It turned out that the man had a record of 51 arrests and was on the wanted list for having jumped bail three times.

What happens when a criminal is finally caught? This happened:

—All our window display merchandise was tied up by the court as evidence.

—Our manager spent one entire day in court, and because the case was not reached, he lost half the next day.

—Ditto for the policeman.

—Despite the defendant's history, the District Attorney bargained with him to plead guilty to a lesser cime.

—Despite the fact that the man had jumped bail three times, the judge granted him bail again—making him free to conduct business as usual.

Is it possible that we can fly to the moon but can't cope with crime in the streets?[11]

Finally, mention might be made of a terse three-line communication to the paper that, in its way, summarizes all the foregoing letters: "Crime," it notes, "will not decrease until being a criminal becomes more dangerous than being a victim."[12]

These letters, of course, are by no means representative. They come from New York City where citizens have a defined and, perhaps, real crime problem, which is more aggravated than in most cities and which may add a certain acerbity to the tone of the letters. That they appear in the paper at all indicates their origin with persons accustomed to making strong opinions known at large. The *Times* itself probably intruded some bias; there was a sharp upsurge in letters such as these during 1971 and then an obvious diminution thereafter. Perhaps the paper began to receive fewer such letters, though, more likely, it merely ceased to broadcast the same refrain. It seems worth marking, however, the manner in which the writers sometimes agitate against offenders not out of patently retributive impulses, but because they feel that the victim's position has been derogated vis-à-vis the criminal's. It would be worth knowing, among other things, how better attention to the cares and needs of the crime victim might bring about more compassionate concern with the welfare of the offender.

The Crime Victim and the Police

It is possible to discover some relatively clear patterns of responses by crime victims to most functionaries in the criminal justice system. The foregoing letters, for instance, indicate a hostility to court processes and personnel that is found among virtually all crime victims. There is a very wide range of opinion in regard to the police, however, among victims. Most generally, persons who suffer property losses tend to complain that the police act in an apathetic, perfunctory manner toward them. The police appear to be regarded much more sympathetically by victims of violence, especially by women (except, of course, for rape victims, whose true victimization the police notoriously tend to regard as unlikely[13]). Apart from emotional distinctions between reactions to personal and property victimization, it is probable that the police find in the much higher prospect of solving personal offenses considerable encouragement for rapport, since officers and victim can link up in a successful endeavor to get the offender, and later can join forces in collaborative scorn for the "indulgence" of the criminal by other segments of the criminal justice mechanism.

An illustration of victim disenchantment with the police appears in a newspaper interview with a Washington, D.C., man who had been forced into an alley at knife point and then robbed of his watch, credit cards, $1200 ring, and $80 in cash. He reported the police performance this way:

They were useless. All they did was to take down my story and ask me questions about it, like I was the robber or something. They wouldn't even go back to where it happened to get the guy's fingerprints, which were all over my wallet and the cellophane. In the end one of them said, "Why were you carrying so much money?" and that was the end of it. He didn't even say goodnight. It happened two weeks ago, and I haven't seen them since.[14]

Considerable insight into the dynamics of victim-police interaction is offered by a Los Angeles man, who was scared out of his wits by robbers who pushed their way into his house and trussed him at gunpoint and then left with his stereo and other valuables:

Police, being used to hearing lots of horror tales, are rarely impressed. They also feel the quite reasonable need to inject some calm into the situation. The details that make the story real merely slow down the average cop who wants to get his job done and his report written or, possibly, get some relevant information out on the radio, usually information like the description you cannot provide.[15]

The remarks of an apartment owner in New York are quite different, as she identifies the police as her protectors and castigates those who she believes are handcuffing them from doing the kind of job she presumes they are interested in. She had been mugged three times during the previous three years, once by a 17-year-old girl and twice by boys no more than 12-years old:

. . . the police is not allowed to do nothing! This mayor of ours, he stopped the police from doing anything to the Negroes and the Spanish. The president, what did he do yet to let the police go? I tell you something—if the cops would take their sticks and give a good beating to these lousy kids the first time they do something wrong, they wouldn't do it a second time. But nobody does nothing for the white folks—only they do for the others.[16]

This recourse to "racial" explanations of crime victim-system interaction, incidentally, is something that took us rather by surprise in our own interviews, because it occurred so often. Perhaps our startlement merely indicates our own encapsulation from persons and circles among whom criminal behavior is commonplace, though it may point to a need to resolve more satisfactorily victim difficulties as an important step toward ameliorating in some ways broader racial problems in our society. Apparently, smoldering resentments and bigotry are given full rein when a victim feels thwarted by the criminal justice process. A San Francisco truck driver, for instance, who was stabbed 17 times by a black man he said he never saw before (our best guess is that they earlier had exchanged words in a liquor store and that the assailant followed the victim to the parking lot of a supermarket to which he was making a delivery) ranted about the fact that courts are disinterested in "bringing people to justice" and insisted that the assailant's witnesses were given priority over his because "niggers are running the country now." As long as the person who stabbed him was "a nigger," he said, "nothing will be done."

A 66-year-old woman, beaten into unconsciousness and raped in her bedroom by an intruder, thought that her problem in part was associated with the fact that "the colored race is trying to get that 'black power' going." "They should have equal rights," she said, "but they are going about it wrong." Along the way, she also threw in the idea that one of the things causing trouble was that "Mexicans can get a license to drive without reading or writing." This victim illustrated, at the same time, the fact that a simplistic view about the relationship between injury from crime and what can be called anti-liberal impulses do not always prevail. Thus, though she went on at some length about the need for "whipping posts so that people can see who the criminals are," this woman was even more insistent that laws against prostitution had to be repealed in order to protect persons like herself. This latter view, she insisted firmly, was a total reversal of the attitude that she had held before the victimization episode.

Crime Victims and the Courts

The shuffling about of the crime victim during court processes is notorious. Astute defense attorneys devote a good deal of time and ingenuity to disconcerting, hazing, and otherwise making the victim of crime miserable. Clearly, this latter is a fundamental element of the adversary system of criminal justice, and perhaps it is part of the slag that is unfortunately essential in order to produce a reasonably pure product. Such philosophical speculations, however, do little to alleviate the malaise of the crime victim. Consider, for example, the position of a victim of a mugging—a person who has already run up a drawerfull of hospital bills and missed days or weeks of work because of the criminal incident—who is cross-examined by a defense attorney operating in accord with the following advice offered in a standard book on trial tactics:

When you have forced the witness into giving you a direct answer to your question you really have him under control; he is off-balance, and usually rather scared. This advantage should be followed up with a few simple questions, such as, "You did not want to answer that question, did you?" If the witness says that he wanted to answer it, ask him in a resounding voice, "Well, why did you not answer it when I first asked you?" Whatever his answer is, you then ask him, "Did you think that you were smart enough to evade answering the question?" Again, whatever the answer is you ask him, "Well, I would like for the jurors to know what you have behind all this dodging and ducking you have done!" ... This battering and legal-style "kicking the witness around" not only humiliates but subdues him.[17]

The position of the crime victim in court has been examined by Richard H. Kuh, newly appointed district attorney in Manhattan, on the basis of a decade of experience as a prosecutor. "What is nearest and dearest to the heart of the victim of crime?" Kuh asks rhetorically and goes on to answer.

... equal standing in the criminal courts to the standing of the defendant in a criminal case, and by that I mean something very simple, and that is the right of the complainant, when it comes to such things as adjournments, appearances in court, to be entitled to some consideration.
I have seen complainants scolded and harassed by judges, and I will say by prosecutors, including myself, and when they have said to us, "I will not come down again, I have been here twelve times and every time I am here there is some reason for an adjournment, and I cannot miss any more days of work. I just will not come again."
And I as a prosecutor have had—and I might say it is the most hateful thing I have done in my years of prosecution—I have had the problem of telling these complainants we have no alternative but to hold you in contempt if you don't come down again.[18]

When he was appointed to succeed Frank S. Hogan as district attorney early in 1974, one of Kuh's first moves was to establish regional offices throughout the borough so that crime victims could more easily register their complaints.[19] Whether Kuh will institute further changes in order to be responsive to his own awareness of the plight of the crime victim will be worth watching.

Attitudes of crime victims toward the courts are typified, though in slightly stronger form, in an interview we had with a Lamont, California, victim who had been shot in the back when he was leaving the scene where had had been involved in a drinking dispute:

His lawyers and the D.A. were in court. The D.A. dropped the charges from shooting with attempt to commit murder to assault and battery. When I heard this I left the courtroom. He was given only 150 days . . . I don't think it was right and neither does the police. The chief wrote an article for the newspaper about it.

Both the court situation and the earlier problem of crime victims with the police have also been noted by Donald E. Santarelli, director of the Law Enforcement Assistance Administration. A newspaper report on a speech by Santarelli to state and city officials sums up his concerns:

The policeman says, "You be down at the stationhouse at 9 o'clock tomorrow night for the lineup." The victim wonders: Where's the stationhouse? Where's the lineup? How do I get there? Is it in the ghetto? Is it at night when I don't want to go out?
You take it to the courthouse, where it really becomes a hassle. The typical witness room looks like the waiting room in a mental hospital.
A prosecution witness may find himself next to the defendant's mother-in-law with her big umbrella . . . . and every kook and nut and friend of the addict, junkie, and arrestee.
More often than not, you find a clash occurring and the witness is just scared to death and that's the end of the case. The testimony suddenly becomes very unclear.[20]

Survivors of Homicide Victims

The foregoing materials can be supplemented with the results of a survey of survivors of homicide victims in regard to their attitudes toward criminal justice processes conducted by Shirley Blumberg with ten persons in southern California during 1972 as a class project.[21] She came to the following conclusions:

1. In cases in which there has been a final court disposition, all survivors except one reported some dissatisfaction with the courts. The exception was a case in which the offender is permanently paralyzed from a policeman's bullet in his spine. Statements such as, "The courts were too lenient," "He didn't get what he deserved; he deserved the death penalty," and "They should spend the rest of their lives in prison" were common. Plea bargaining was uniformly condemned on the ground that it resulted in undeservedly light sentences. Laziness of prosecutors and crowded court calendars were blamed for the reductions in charges.

2. In response to questions about causes of crime or attitudes toward the killer, eight of ten respondents adhered to a medical model of explanation. They repeatedly said, "He was obviously sick," "I know it had to be a sick mind," and "They were sick; they had to be." Early identification of deviant behavior with subsequent mental treatment was suggested by several persons as the best cure for crime. "In school, when they see behavior like that develop, they should catch it. They should refer him to an analyst or something," one person

said. Another stated: "Families who become cognizant that one of their children deviates from the normal should seek help. They shouldn't be ashamed of it or try to hide it. They should seek help right away."

3. In all cases, general attitudes toward the police depended upon the amount and kind of attention given by the law enforcement officer to the survivor. When the police called on a family member and kept him informed of progress in the case, attitudes were invariably friendly. When the police did not make or keep friendly contact, the survivor harbored bitter feelings. In one case, the police did not inform the parents of their son's death; rather, a witness to the crime told them about it a day later. In another instance, the survivor is angry with the police, understandably enough, because they suspected him at first of having killed his wife. Still another respondent has always enjoyed good, cooperative relations with the police, but he says he is now disturbed because they appear to be "dragging their feet."

4. In response to the inquiry, "Do you think politicians care about crime, or can control it?" the respondents uniformly exhibited a combination of goodwill and skepticism toward politicians. Answers included the cynical observation of a 23-year-old Mexican-American: "They don't want crime to go on, but when it doesn't happen to them, it's just all statistics." A 63-year-old widow said: "If they cared enough, they could do something. There's just too many things they care about more." A 62-year-old widower thought that "They could do something, but won't unless it helps keep them in power."

Several case vignettes flesh out the above conclusions:

The respondent was the mother of a 17-year-old girl who had been dumped in an alley after being given enough barbiturates to kill her. Evidence was not conclusive as to whether she had been alive at the time she was abandoned. Following a plea bargain, two young men pled guilty to voluntary manslaughter. A third received a lesser sentence for agreeing to testify for the state. The mother is extremely bitter toward the offenders, the courts, and society in general. She believes that the case constituted first-degree murder and that sentences of 1 to 15 years are totally inadequate. She reports that her family has disintegrated since the incident. Her oldest child, a 19-year-old daughter, no longer speaks to her. A 10-year-old son has been sent to Colorado to attend private school. The mother says she is fearful for her 3-year-old son. She believes that the city environment could turn him toward drugs. She would like to leave, but feels that she can't afford it. Her grief, she says, is still acute; she reports that she "bleeds all the time. It gets worse and worse."

The survivor, a realtor came home one evening and discovered that his wife and been strangled, beaten, and shot in the back of the head. There was no sign of a struggle and nothing was missing except some coins from a piggy bank. There has not been an arrest. The husband was under suspicion at first but was cleared after taking a lie detector test. The initial police suspicion plus what the survivor believes is a lack of interest in the case on the part of the police has led this politically conservative man to a feeling of bitterness toward the police. He blames general permissiveness and lack of discipline in today's society for crime. His wife's sister has become convinced that he killed the wife, and this had led to a rift between the families. Because the police suspect that his wife was killed by someone she knew, the husband finds himself looking at his acquaintances with suspicion.

The body of a 59-year-old psychiatric nurse who died of asphyxiation during a rape attempt was discovered by the respondent, her daughter. Her mother's hands were bound and a pillowcase was over her head. She had a nasal obstruction from a previous injury, and was unable to breathe with a gag stuffed into her mouth. The daughter believes the man did not intend to murder. The suspect, believed to have committed at least 24 rapes, was captured following another rape attempt. He escaped from jail and fled to Illinois. Two years later, while breaking into a house, he was shot in the spine by police and is now permanently paralyzed. Following extradition, he was convicted of rape and of breaking and entering. The daughter is satisfied; she believes that a lifetime paralysis is worse than life imprisonment and "he got what's coming to him." She would like to see him brought to trial for her mother's death, though, so that the case "can be closed." She feels that the offender is sick and should have had treatment when he was younger.

A 21-year-old Chicano was visiting some friends. In the apartment with him were two young women, a baby, and another man. There was an intrusion by two other men who were high on pills. During a squabble, one of the intruders slipped or was pushed down the stairs. He reported this to his 30-year-old brother who returned to the scene with an automatic rifle and began firing into the room from the doorway. One injured man staggered outside, was taken to a hospital, and survived. The other died 15 minutes after being hit. The respondent, the decedent's 23-year-old brother, thinks quicker action could have saved his brother's life. He reports that the police did not inform his parents of the murder, although they arrested the killer immediately. He is particularly bitter toward the courts. In spite of several eye witnesses, the District Attorney reduced the charge to second-degree murder, and the offender was sentenced to 5 years to life. The brother asks: "If this isn't cold-blooded murder, what is?" He has purchased a gun so that he will not, he says, be unprepared like his brother was. He believes that the murderer, whom he knew only slightly, was always "mean" and "goofy." He reports that his mother has changed; she's now very quiet and sad.

Perhaps it needs to be indicated, in summary, that the purpose here is not to adjudicate the fairness of the treatment accorded the offenders in these cases. Justice may indeed have been served in all instances. The interviews show, however, a seething and deep discontent in many of the survivors of victims of violent crime. To the extent that these feelings exist, some part of the criminal justice system seems to have failed to do as much as could have been done to see to it that the victimized were comforted and dealt with more satisfactorily in their distress.

Conclusions

Two conclusions emerge from our materials:

First, it is fortunate for the functionaries in the adjudication stage in the criminal justice system that they have a monopoly on the administration of justice. Rarely has a group been so uniformly regarded with so little respect, much less admiration, by those with whom they do business. That there are important consequences of this low esteem seems undeniable: it is probably reflected in crime reporting rates, in local and national elections, in patriotism quotients, and in similar significant ways.

Second, it is fortunate for the same functionaries that those who they offend tend, as crime victims, to be among the most powerless and least articulate persons within the society. Insulated on high, judges are grandly protected from the disparagement that so routinely was divulged to us by the crime victims whose cases the courts handled. Blumberg clearly portrays the in-group camaraderie and clubbiness that marks the work of officials in the criminal justice system and excludes the participants in the process from access to or retaliation against wrongs they feel they have suffered.[22] In their private lives, the officials generally mingle to a large extent with persons who never have reason to experience the indifference that the lower class, who constitute the vast number of crime victims, maintain that they receive.

Given these conclusions, what can be done? The following are but a few of the remedial steps that ought to be considered:

1. Somebody has to be designated to see that victims get a fairer shake, if only in the name of public relations. A letter informing them of the disposition of their case, thanking them for their cooperation, explaining to them what will go on or what has gone on would be a minimum fulfillment of the dictates of courtesy and consideration.

2. Somebody has to attend to scheduling that takes into account inconveniences to the victim and sees to it that adequate compensation, at a minimum, is accorded to citizens who suffer losses through court appearances and postponements.

3. Systems of victim compensation[23] that include not only medical and loss-of-earning reparations, but also social service assistance, vocational advice, and encouragement—not as charity, but as the right of a citizen in need—should be mounted and expanded.

4. Scholars must turn further attention to the plight of the crime victim. We need more information on what it means to be a criminal victim. What are the costs and other consequences? How about the "labeling" of the victim, by physical injury or psychological trauma from criminal activity directed against him or her? On the basis of such research and much more careful thought than has been given to the subject until now, new programs bringing justice and decency to crime victims must be inaugurated.

Notes

1. The interview was conducted by Dorothy Zietz, professor of social work, California State University, Sacramento.

2. For an overview of the field see Israel Drapkin and Emilio Viano, editors, *Victimology* (Lexington, Mass.: D.C. Heath, 1974).

3. See, generally, Robert Lejeune and Nicholas Alex, "On Being Mugged: The Event and Its Aftermath," *Urban Life and Culture* 2 (1973):259-287. See also Carl Bernstein, "Fear Haunts Holdup Victims: Mental Stress May Overshadow Physical Harm," *Washington Post*, September 5, 1970.

4. David Epstein, quoted in Ivan G. Goldman, "Crime is Just the Start of Victims' Difficulties," *Washington Post*, June 6, 1971.

5. President's Commission on Law Enforcement and Administration of Justice, *Task Force Report—Assessment of Crime* (Washington: Government Printing Office, 1967), p. 80.

6. Robert D. Childres, "Compensation for Criminally Inflicted Personal Injury," *New York University Law Review* 39 (1964):471.

7. Joseph A. Silverman, Letter to the Editor, *The New York Times*, November 15, 1971. Reprinted by permission of Dr. Silverman.

8. For a particularly sophisticated statement on this subject, see Sidney Hook, "The Rights of the Victim: Thoughts on Crime and Compassion," *Encounter* 38 (1972):11-15.

9. William A. Conway, Letter to the Editor, *The New York Times*, November 2, 1971. Reprinted by permission of Mr. Conway.

10. A.G. Hanau, Letter to the Editor, *The New York Times*, August 2, 1971. Reprinted by permission of Mr. Hanau.

11. Mortimer Levitt, Letter to the Editor, *The New York Times*, December 18, 1971. Reprinted by permission of Mr. Levitt.

12. Donald A. Windsor, Letter to the Editor, *The New York Times*, December 8, 1971. Reprinted by permission of Mr. Windsor.

13. Susan Griffin, "Rape: The All-American Crime," *Ramparts* 10 (1971):26-36, is a good representative of a considerable literature to this point.

14. Quoted in Tom Wolff, "Pain, Terror Concealed in Reports of Muggings," *Los Angeles Times*, December 14, 1972.

15. Charles T. Powers, " 'Say One Word and I'll Cut Your Throat,' " *Los Angeles Times*, January 13, 1974.

16. Morton Hunt, *The Mugging* (New York: New American Library, 1973), p. 394. I have put Hunt's attempt to capture phonetically the landlady's German-English back into plain English.

17. Lewis W. Lake, *How to Win Lawsuits Before Juries* (New York: Prentice-Hall, 1954), pp. 164-65.

18. New York, Meeting of the Governor's Committee on the Compensation of Victims of Violent Crime, January 14, 1966, pp. 37-38.

19. "Kuh is Sworn In: Plans Neighborhood D.A. Offices," *The New York Times*, February 14, 1974.

20. "Aid Sought for Crime Victims," *Los Angeles Times* (AP), January 14, 1974.

21. Shirley Blumberg, "The Survivors: Attitudes of Families of Homicide

Victims," unpublished seminar paper, Program in Social Ecology, University of California, Irvine, December 8, 1972.

22. Abraham S. Blumberg, *Criminal Justice* (Chicago: Quadrangle, 1967).

23. See, generally, Herbert Edelhertz and Gilbert Geis, *Public Compensation to Victims of Crime* (New York: Praeger, 1974).

6

Compensating Victims of Violent Crime

Herbert Edelhertz

In the modern era our concern about violent crime seems to flag when we come closer to considering what we can do for the victims of crime in a direct, personal, and material way. This is in contrast to ancient times, or to the practices of primitive societies, in which means of compensation to crime victims or their survivors were seen as practical steps necessary to preserve order or further other community objectives.[1] While sporadic voices on behalf of compensating crime victims were to be heard in the nineteenth century and the first half of the twentieth century, the current movement to compensate crime victims should be dated from the pioneering work that Margaret Fry launched in 1957 in Great Britain.[2]

As we look back to 1957, we can see revolutionary change. Instead of a few voices crying in the wilderness, programs to compensate crime victims are delivering benefits in Great Britain, Sweden, Australia, New Zealand, and Canada. In the United States, victims are receiving meaningful benefits in Massachusetts, New York, New Jersey, Maryland, California, Hawaii, and the State of Washington. New programs have been launched in Alaska, Illinois, and Louisiana. Programs exist in Nevada and Georgia that at least give lip service to the principle that victims of violent crime should be compensated, and there are strongly supported efforts in the United States Congress to enact federal legislation that would encourage and financially support state programs to compensate crime victims.

One is tempted to speculate on the reasons why we have been so late in coming to assume societal responsibility to compensate victims of violent crime, and why we are moving so grudgingly in this direction.

Obviously, the major reason is that compensating crime victims costs money, which means competition for a share of the dollar. If we look at the plight of the victim in a social welfare context, it is difficult to give him priority over the sick and the needy. Most victims will fail to qualify for assistance on welfare grounds until they have destituted themselves. If we look at the plight of the victim in the context of the criminal justice system, there are competing demands for dollars that are backed by broader and more powerful constituencies: enforcement fraternities and those concerned with correction and rehabilitation of offenders. Until very recently, the social science community contributed little to the movement to directly help crime victims; it has been more intellectually engaging to consider such issues as victim proneness (finding ways to put some blame on victims)[a] or to try to abate crime by seeking "root causes."

The victim of crime has not been a customer of the criminal justice system, or a recognized category of our welfare system. Change is taking place. We see not only the victim compensation movement but also the emerging concern with rape victims—who would probably still be ignored if their plight were not of interest to the womens' movement, which provides a broader supporting constituency.

Whatever the reasons, there is a tide of support for direct aid to victims. The strength of the tide is politically recognized by legislators, who can more and more identify with the sentiments of one member of the British House of Lords. In debate preceding enactment of the British Program, this peer said:

> I do not think I am guilty of wild or extravagant language or unnecessary hyperbole if I say that the popularity of the Government is not at the moment at its zenith. Fervent supporters of the Government such as myself frequently pray that the Government should be given more chances to do something which is both popular and right. My Lords, here is their chance.[3]

This tide is likely to continue to flow and to result in legislation of national scope. We should, therefore, consider the philosophies that underlie victim compensation, the kinds of programs that result from such philosophies, and the options available to jurisdictions that elect to provide direct assistance to crime victims.

Rationale for Compensating Crime Victims

Two principal reasons are usually given for enacting victim compensation legislation.

The first is that government has the obligation to protect its citizens and that, failing this, it has a duty to provide compensation for its failure to provide adequate protection. One might characterize this as a part of the *social contract* theory. Subsumed within it are other elements—for example, we have surrendered our right to private vengeance or to arming ourselves for private defense—that are all in reliance on the implicit or explicit promises or entreaties of the organized community.

The second reason is that crime is unavoidable in our society and that its impacts or burdens should be borne by society generally rather than solely by

---

[a]Samuel Butler, in his *Erewhon* described a "Utopian" society in which the victim of crime, not the perpetrator, was prosecuted. Victims of crime, the needy, and the ill are, after all, a material burden, and their plight makes the rest of us uncomfortable. In Erewhon, they were all prosecuted and jailed.

those who unfortunately are chance selections for victimization. This might be called an *insurance* theory. In World War II Britain, those whose property was destroyed by German bombs were compensated by the general community on a similar theory, and I believe it has much to recommend it. Consider the similarity: those who lived in London or near factories, ports, or military installations were more likely to be bombed. In the United States, the risk is clearly greater for those who, through no fault of their own, are poor or black and live in or near ghetto areas. Within high risk areas, in wartime Britain or today's American cities, the selection of victims is basically unrelated to personal fault.[b] "There but for the grace of God go I" is another, and a good way to make the point that individuals should not have to assume costs imposed on them by society, without help.

A third reason is sometimes given for aiding crime victims—that is, they need help. This is the welfare rationale which was the basis for the original California victim compensation program (recently scrapped for a more equitable compensation structure), and its influence can usually be seen in other programs.

These rationale directly influence the drafting of victim compensation legislation. If one looks to the social contract theory, benefits are a matter of right. Limitations on personal eligibility or extent of benefits are less compatible with this theory. If one looks to the insurance theory, one is more likely to think in terms of contributory fault or more readily accept limitations of liability. If one looks to or is influenced by the welfare theory, one is more likely to require some showing of financial need.

It would be naive to believe that victim compensation programs are developed within strictly defined theoretical frameworks. In practice, these and other theories merge and together with other political and economic factors determine the shape of a program. Sometimes these theories are considered and then discarded, and the programs that are established give the illusion but not the substance of responsibility to compensate victims. Examples are the "Good Samaritan" program in Nevada or the Georgia program that seems structured to avoid paying victims.[c]

Benefits Provided

Comprehensive programs in the United States generally provide limited benefits to limited classes of victims. Since these programs pay only for medical expenses

[b]I do not ignore the issue of victim proneness, but would suggest that a victim-prone individual is more likely to come to grief in a ghetto than in an affluent neighborhood.

[c]The Georgia program was enacted in 1967. As of 1973, no awards were made. Considering the statute and its implementing machinery, I would doubt anything has been paid during the last year.

and loss of earnings,[d] the greater part of our population is excluded from benefits because of bars to "double recovery." A victim who has $1,000 in medical expenses covered by medical insurance and who is paid his wages while incapacitated, but uses up his sick leave in the process, is entitled to nothing. If his medical insurance provides for a $50 deductible, he will not even be entitled to $50, since victim compensation programs usually provide for deductibles or minimums that bar small claims.

If one is truly needy, these programs are almost worthless. The victim on welfare can show no loss of earnings, and medical costs are not compensable because the victim is eligible through welfare medical programs such as Medicaid. One who has medical insurance or sick leave must exhaust such benefits before becoming eligible for compensation.

As a general rule, therefore, these programs will only benefit limited groups: those who are not too poor and those who do not have insurance or other benefits to pay medical expenses or prevent interruptions of income.

For those who are eligible, benefits are often inadequate. Most states set maximum limits of $10,000. The highest maximum is $45,000 (Maryland), although New York allows unlimited reimbursement for actual medical expenses. The State of Washington has no maximum, but limitations are those of its state workmen's compensation program. Proposed federal legislation is somewhat more generous; it would provide for a $50,000 maximum.

We should give much consideration to a new approach to the nature and extent of benefits to be provided for such programs. There are inequities in the bar to "double recovery" in that it penalizes those with the foresight to buy insurance or give up other employment benefits to get such insurance as a fringe. Politically this inequity will be difficult to eliminate, and its elimination should not be a high priority effort. More important should be efforts to liberalize maximum benefits, to provide compensation for permanent injuries and pain and suffering (outside Hawaii a rape victim will get nothing for her trauma), and to consider the elimination of deductibles or requirements that claims exceed some minimum amount. While such deductibles and minimums may be administratively justifiable (the costs of processing can exceed the amount of possible awards), amounts under $100 may be very important to low-income claimants.

Who Is Eligible for Compensation

As a general rule, only victims of violent crime or those who suffer injuries when they go to the aid of a victim or law enforcement officer are eligible to receive

---

[d]The only exception in the United States is Hawaii, which will provide limited compensation for "pain and suffering." In Great Britain, the situation is quite the opposite; there is a broad social welfare system to provide medical services and compensate for loss of wages, and the program can award substantial sums for common-law damages, including pain and suffering.

compensation. Victims may be denied compensation or be given only partial compensation if they are found to have provoked assault, are guilty of contributory fault, or fail to cooperate with law enforcement authorities in connection with a prosecution. It is not necessary that the offender be apprehended, charged, or convicted.

Invariably excluded are victims married to or engaged in voluntary sexual relations with the offender as are children or other dependents of the offender. The reasons usually given for these exclusions are that offenders should not be allowed to indirectly benefit from their crimes and that it is often difficult to determine the degree of provocation or contributory fault by victims in domestic settings. The real reason is probably that a very substantial portion of violent crimes take place in such domestic settings, and the exclusion from benefits of these victims is believed to greatly lower the costs of victim compensation programs. While the cost picture is not clear, these ostensible reasons will not withstand critical analysis and are patently unjust.

What is meant by an "indirect benefit" to the offender? In legislative committees considering victim compensation programs, these examples are given: If a man shoots his wife, he will be benefitted to the extent that the state takes over his obligation of support and medical payments. If a man kills his wife thereby leaving destitute children with no mother to support and care for them, he will be benefitted to the extent that the state takes over his obligation to support her (or her and his) children. In the real world, this father or husband or lover will be relieved of nothing; he will be sitting in jail. Only the victim or the victim's dependents will suffer from this exclusion, not the offender.

The fundamental inequity of the familial exclusion is clearly demonstrated in one case reported by the Maryland Criminal Injuries Compensation Board:

Claim filed on behalf of the two infant claimants by their mother. Claimants' mother was first wife of their father, the victim. Claimants' father was shot and killed by his second wife, the infants' stepmother. Section 5(6)(b) and 2(d)(1) of Article 26A of the Maryland Annotated Code together exclude members of the family of a person who is criminally responsible for a crime of becoming eligible to receive an award under out statute. Since the infant claimants are within the third degree of affinity to the assailant, we find the infants not to be eligible to receive an award growing out of this claim. The claim is, therefore, disallowed.

Determining whether the offender and victim were sexually involved with each other at the time of the crime is not always easy. The difficulty is illustrated by a British case that the Criminal Injuries Compensation Board described as follows:

A girl, aged 19, became friendly with a man, and he came to stay at her grandmother's house where she was then living. She and her grandmother shared a bedroom while the man slept in the backroom. They went away on holidays together . . . registered as man and wife. . . . On the way home in the train she told him she wanted no more to do with him. It was agreed that he should return with her to her grandmother's house, have a meal and then leave by train. After the meal he attacked the girl and her grandmother with a hatchet. Both the grandmother and the girl received full award; the girl because her relationship . . . was a casual one which had come to an end . . . in the train.

The technical legal argument that in domestic situations it will be difficult to determine whether the victim provoked the assault or was in some degree contributorily at fault is not persuasive. Tribunals are often faced with the task of making difficult fact decisions, and they would undoubtedly exercise discretion to require a more substantial degree of proof with respect to crimes arising from domestic conflicts. It should also be noted that convictions in such cases are not uncommon; provocations are rarely held to justify one party resorting to a knife or gun.

The familial exclusion, not withstanding its inequity, provokes little critical comment on the part of scholars or administrators of victim compensation programs. The situation is quite different with respect to the requirement that victims show some degree of need for assistance in order to be eligible. The so-called "needs test" is almost uniformly condemned by program administrators and others familiar with the operation of such programs. Support for the needs test seems confined to legislators who adopt the welfare rationale for such programs or who wish to limit the costs of these programs. There is considerable doubt that money is saved by imposition of such needs tests.

Among the more comprehensive programs that have been in operation for a reasonable period of time, those in Massachusetts, New Jersey, and Hawaii impose no needs test; the ones in New York and Maryland require a showing of "serious financial hardship" that stops short of compelling a victim to exhaust his assets to the point of impoverishment in order to qualify for benefits. While no scientific analysis of claimants and claims has been made, it seems highly unlikely that even a small handful of successful claimants in Massachusetts, New Jersey, or Hawaii would have been ineligible under New York or Maryland rules. The major impact of these "needs tests" would seem to be to subject claimants to a demeaning claim procedure and a harassing investigation focusing on the victim's financial status rather than on compensable damages inflicted on the victim.

The New York Crime Compensation Board made no bones about its attitude toward this distasteful requirement in its 1970 Report:

The most difficult problem still continues to be determining the question of serious financial hardship. Many of the elderly people who are retired, who have worked many years, have been frugal and have saved money to take care of them in their declining years represent one group that the Board feels should be reimbursed for their medical expenses. However, the statute makes no distinction and, therefore, if they have substantial savings the statute does not permit an award to these elderly persons.

Another segment of our society is the middle-income man who has supported his family, has been gainfully employed, and is not only a respectable but responsible citizen. This claimant feels that having been a law-abiding citizen who has worked hard and paid taxes, he is entitled to receive his unreimbursed medical expenses and his loss of earnings within the limitations allowed by the statute. The Board continues to feel that these two classes of individuals should be compensated.

The chief investigator for the New York Board has estimated that elimination of the New York needs test would add about 10 percent to the costs of that program. It is questionable whether it would add anything at all. It costs more than $200 to administer each claim processed in New York. More work goes into checking financial eligibility data than any other claim element, and it is the area in which accurate information is much harder to get. Each claim is investigated with respect to this requirement; it is not a situation in which there is a presumption of regularity buttressed by spot check audits as in the case of income tax. In all probability, it costs more to administer a needs test than a jurisdiction saves by requiring it. It also appears that much of what little fraudulent activity has been observed in victim compensation programs has been in response to such needs tests.

It is regrettable that proposed federal legislation follows the model of the New York statute in requiring a test of financial need as a basis for subventing the costs of state programs.

Administrative Machinery for
Deliverying Victim Compensation

There are three basic patterns for administering the payment of compensation to victims of violent crime.

1. *An independent administrative agency with no other function can be established to deliver victim compensation.* This is how programs are administered in New York, Maryland, New Jersey, and Hawaii. It is also the British pattern.

2. *Courts can be employed to decide and make awards to victims.* In the United States, only Massachusetts employs this model. The Massachusetts Attorney General's office is charged with responsibility for investigating claims and representing the state in court. The district courts almost invariably accept the recommendations of the Massachusetts Attorney General.

3. *Delivery of victim compensation can be made through existing workmen's compensation programs.* Most Canadian programs operate in this way. In the United States, only the State of Washington employs this model.

Both independent agencies and workmen's compensation boards seem capable of efficient and compassionate administration of these programs. There is some doubt whether the same can be said for the judicial model employed in Massachusetts.[4]

Costs of Victim Compensation Programs

Comparatively little is known about what a well run, comprehensive program would cost. We do know the costs of existing programs, but these figures may be misleading since there is reason to believe that many, if not most, of those who would be eligible to make claims are not aware of the existence of programs that could compensate them.

One study conducted by the Law Enforcement Assistance Administration of the U.S. Department of Justice estimated that—based on the experience of New York and Maryland—it would cost between $22 and $24 million in 1974 to pay 75 percent of the costs of nationwide state programs with a $50,000 maximum and a financial hardship test for victims; this estimate is regarded as much too low in a subsequent L.E.A.A. analysis based on other assumptions.

It seems evident that well-publicized programs, administered in a manner that would find and encourage eligible victims to file claims, would be far more costly than the original L.E.A.A. estimate. The Chairman of the New York Board pointed out that his program cost less than 2 percent of the amount budgeted for institutional care of offenders in his state. Effective and compassionate aid to victims of crime should be worth double the price.

Future Prospects

The movement toward establishing new programs to compensate victims of violent crime has been moving forward steadily in the states. The principal barrier has been financial, and there would appear to be little chance for coverage in every state in the absence of federal support. The Congress seems well on its way toward providing such support in the near future.

Former Senator Ralph Yarborough of Texas gave the original impetus to the movement for federal legislation in the U.S. Congress. His efforts were continued, after his departure from the Senate, by Senator Mike Mansfield of Montana and Senator John L. McClellan of Arkansas. The Senate has overwhelmingly approved victim compensation legislation on several occasions, but these laws failed to get out of committee in the House of Representatives. The situation seems to be changing. The new chairman of the House Judiciary Committee, Congressman Peter W. Rodino, Jr., of New Jersey, has introduced his own bill and held hearings on it.

Proposed federal bills seem to fall into a common pattern. They would establish compensation programs in the District of Columbia and federal enclaves that would be patterned roughly on the New York model, provide for a $50,000 maximum, and vest administrative jurisdiction in a board within the Law Enforcement Assistance Administration of the U.S. Department of Justice. At the same time, state programs would be encouraged by grants-in-aid that would cover 75 percent of award costs and costs of administration of state programs, to the extent that their benefits would be co-extensive with those proposed for the federal program in the District of Columbia.

This proposed federal legislation can pose many serious problems, both legal and financial, for state programs. A jurisdiction that does not impose a needs test might have to demonstrate that each claimant given an award would have been eligible under the federal needs test; 75 percent reimbursement for the award amount and perhaps for administrative costs related thereto would depend on such a showing.

Notwithstanding these and other problems, it is likely that something close to presently projected federal legislation will be enacted, which will undoubtedly generate responsive legislative activity in state legislatures throughout the country. Rhode Island established an abortive program in 1972, which was to become effective within 120 days from the date of enactment of the federal legislation that had been anticipated in that year but never passed the House of Representatives. Few state legislatures will be able to withstand pressure to enact programs if the federal government pays 75 percent of the costs.

Conclusion

Commentators have characterized victim compensation as "an idea whose time has come." New programs in several states, activities in the U.S. Congress, and increasing public and criminal justice system attention to the plight of crime victims would indicate the correctness of this view. For those who are truly concerned with the plight of the victim, it is essential that efforts be directed toward programs that do more than just deliver compensation. The effort must be to ensure adequacy, fairness, and compassion in these programs.

Notes

1. Cyrus H. Gordon, *Hammurabi's Code: Quaint or Forward-Looking?* (New York: Holt, Rinehart, and Winston, 1960), p. 6. See also Robert F. Harper, *The Code of Hammurabi*, 2nd edition (Chicago: University of Chicago Press, 1904); Arthur Meisel, "The Code of Hammurabi: A Study of Babylonian Courts and Procedure," *Intramural Law Review* 21 (1966):191-223; and J.A. MacCulloch, "Crimes and Punishments—Primitive and Savage," in James Hastings, ed., *Encyclopaedia of Religion and Ethics* (New York: Scribner's, 1951), vol. IV, p. 252. See also Herbert Edelhertz and Gilbert Geis, *Public Compensation to Victims of Crime* (New York: Praeger Publishers, 1974), pp. 7-8.

2. Edelhertz and Geis, ibid., p. 10.

3. Quoted in 245 Parl. Deb. H.L. 260 (1962).

4. For further discussion of these models, see Edelhertz and Geis, *Public Compensation to Victims of Crime*, n. 1.

7

Forcible Rape and the American System of Criminal Justice

Duncan Chappell

As one rather cynical observer of contemporary American reactions to forcible rape has remarked, "Never since the Sabine women were put upon by the Romans has there been as much furor about this crime as in the past year or so."[1]

A variety of factors have sparked and fueled this furor. The crime of forcible rape has received special attention from feminist groups who regard this area of the criminal law as one protecting male property rights, rather than the integrity of a female's body.[2] In the words of Kate Millet, "traditionally rape has been viewed as an offense one male commits upon another—a matter of abusing 'his women.' "[3] According to the feminists, a male-dominated system of criminal justice sustains this attitude by refusing to prosecute or convict all but a handful of rapists.[4] Meanwhile, the victim of rape is subjected to a host of indignities at the hands of the police and other system personnel.

The race of rapists and their victims has been another flash point in the current American debate about forcible rape. The ideological component of interracial forcible rape was cogently expressed by Eldridge Cleaver in *Soul on Ice*:

Rape was an insurrectionary act. It delighted me that I was defying and trampling upon the white man's law, upon his system of values, and that I was defiling his women—and this point, I believe, was the most satisfying to me because I was very resentful over the historical fact of how the white man had used the black women. I felt I was getting revenge.[5]

For a substantial period of American history, the revenge exacted by the white man upon black men who raped white women tended to be death, whether by lynching in earlier times or officially justified execution in more civilized years.[6] It is significant that the recent Supreme Court decision effectively ending capital punishment in the United States involved a black offender sentenced to death for rape.[7] On the other hand, capital punishment for white men raping black women has been virtually unknown in America. Historically, black females were regarded as notably accessible to white men, if not by the choice of the female then by use of force that involved little, if any, likelihood of subsequent penalty.[8]

Quite apart from the controversy swirling around the issues of women's rights, race, the death penalty, and forcible rape, furor about this crime has been further fed by the apparent startling increase in the incidence of this type of violent sexual attack. As Table 7-1 shows, during the past decade forcible rape rates have more than doubled.[a] The pace of increase has become more rapid since 1967; in the early 1970s it reached a speed that has outstripped all other major categories of violent crime. The Uniform Crime Reporting figures indicate that violent crimes as a group increased 1 percent in calender year 1972 over 1971.[9] Forcible rape was up 11 percent, aggravated assault 6 percent, and homicide 4 percent, while the crime of robbery declined 4 percent.

Some American cities reported increases in forcible rape far in excess of the national average. New York City, for instance, recorded a 35 percent rise in reported rapes between 1971 and 1972.[10] A total of 3,271 complaints of rape were made to the New York City Police Department in 1972, which was almost twice the number of complaints made in 1967.

Accounting for and Responding to the "Rape Wave"

For the pundits of criminal statistics facing what has been described by many as a "rape wave," an increase of this magnitude presents some teasing questions.

Table 7-1
Forcible Rape Rates in the United States, 1960-1972

Year	Number	Rate Per 100,000 Inhab.
1960	17,030	9.5
1961	17,060	9.3
1962	17,390	9.4
1963	17,490	9.3
1964	21,230	11.1
1965	23,200	12.0
1966	25,590	13.1
1967	27,380	13.8
1968	31,380	15.7
1969	36,840	18.2
1970	37,650	18.5
1971	41,890	20.3
1972	46,430	22.4[a]

[a]Percent change 1960-1972, 135.8.

Source: Based on data contained in annual volumes of the FBI *Uniform Crime Reports*, 1960-1972.

---

[a]Nationally, for the decade 1960-1970, the number of rapes per 100,000 "eligible females" (excluding those under 5 and those 75 and over) rose from 21.9 in 1960 to 41.3 in 1970.

Does, for instance, the wave represent a real or paper rise in the incidence of forcible rape? Victimization studies have established that the rate of commission of forcible rape in the community far outstrips the reported rate. Estimates of the gap between the two rates vary: the National Victimization Study conducted in 1967 for the President's Crime Commission suggested a ratio of between 3 and 4 actual rapes for each one reported.[11] A more recent Law Enforcement Assistance Administration Pilot Survey in two American cities suggested a two to one ratio, which might possibly indicate a change in victim reporting behavior since 1967.[12] Clearly, a comparatively minor change in this behavior could produce quite a major impact upon the statistics of forcible rape. But the accuracy of victimization studies are themselves open to some doubt, particularly in an area like forcible rape where both subjective and official definitions of the offense tend to vary widely.

Some indication of the variation that occurs in the definition of forcible rape at the official level can be obtained from the results of a recent comparative study the present writer and three colleagues made of police records of this crime in Boston and Los Angeles.[13] The sample of records used in this study were obtained from the National Commission on the Causes and Prevention of Violence and related to forcible rapes reported to the police in the two cities in 1967. At that time, Los Angeles had the dubious distinction of being the rape capital of the nation, while Boston purported to have one of the lowest rape rates in the country.

Our examination of the forcible rape records in Boston and Los Angeles offered very little encouragement for sophisticated comparative study. It became very obvious from our examination that what each department regarded as the kind of case to be classified as forcible rape—and subsequently forwarded to the FBI for inclusion as such in the *Uniform Crime Reports*—was far from equivalent. A far more embrasive definition of what constituted forcible rape prevailed in Los Angeles as contrasted to Boston, and it appears likely that it is this definitional quirk that has for many years placed Los Angeles above the remainder of the nation's cities in its reported rate of forcible rape. Indeed, in Los Angeles, virtually any instance in which a person appeared to be seeking "sexual gratification"—a term favored by that city's detectives—was apt to be classified as a forcible rape. For instance, one case we studied involved a man who sidled up to two young girls on a busy suburban street and then pinched one of them on the bottom. A police officer happened to witness this heinous assault and immediately arrested the man. In a subsequent statement, the offender admitted he frequently engaged in this type of activity, but gained his main satisfaction from frightening the girls. The case was classified by the Los Angeles Police Department as an attempt at forcible rape. Unfortunately, no record of the ultimate disposition of the case was included in the report!

In contrast, to become a forcible rape statistic in Boston, victims seemingly suffered a true "fate worse than death" in compliance with the FBI guidelines that an offense should be classified as forcible rape or attempted forcible rape if it involved actual or attempted sexual intercourse with a female forcibly against her will.[14] This definition excluded specifically cases of statutory rape, in which no force was employed and the victim was under the legal age of consent or otherwise was legally incapacitated from agreeing to participate in the act. Sodomy and incest offenses were also eliminated by definition from the forcible rape category. The classification rules seem reasonably clear. It is another matter, however, to apply the rules carefully and uniformly around the 40,000 or more police forces in the United States.

These comparative observations about police records of forcible rape in two American cities illustrate the dilemmas of drawing any firm conclusions about trends in this category of crime from official statistics. Only when standardized police reporting methods are adopted for forcible rape, and all other major index crimes, are the FBI *Uniform Crime Reports* likely to become of any real assistance. The current absence of such methods, given the nature of public and political concern about crime in the United States, appears almost incomprehensible. Nonetheless, the fact cannot be ignored that whatever the deficiencies of these official statistics, they continue to be the focus of attention in any public or political discussion of the state of crime in the community.

Seeking to assuage public apprehension about the "rape wave," law enforcement officials have implied that much of the increase in this crime may be accounted for by changes in victim reporting behavior and police recording practices. These changes, it has been suggested, are largely the product of the nationwide trend to advance the rights of women, which has resulted in a greater willingness on the part of both victims and police to record rape complaints.[15]

A further factor that may well have influenced recent forcible rape reporting and recording behavior in New York City and allied jurisdictions has been the extensive publicity associated with the liberalization of the New York State law relating to rape. Under the law as it formerly existed, every element of rape had to be corroborated: the identity of an assailant, lack of consent, and penetration.[16] In the absence of an independent witness to a rape or the use of extreme force by an attacker, satisfaction of the corroboration requirements was exceedingly difficult.[17]

Following concerted criticism of the rape law and pressure for change from, among others, feminist groups and the State District Attorney's Association, the New York State Legislature in its 1972 session modified the corroboration requirement for rape.[18] The new law, which came into effect on June 21, 1972, in substance requires that only the victim's testimony of the forcible, non-consensual nature of the rape be corroborated. There need no longer be corroboration of the victim's testimony of penetration or of the assailant's identity. The hope is that this new law will enhance the capacity of the criminal justice system in New York State to cope with the rape problem and this hope may well have been transmitted to victims as well as police and resulted in increased reporting of forcible rapes. Certainly, in the past, the system's performance in the area of rape left much to be desired. In 1972, for instance, only 31 percent of reported rapes were cleared by police in New York City. And "in Manhattan for the first six months of 1971," reported Mayor Lindsay's Criminal Justice Co-Ordinating Council, "only one person received a felony rape sentence. Only thirteen persons charged with felony rape were convicted on any charge."[19]

Modification of New York State laws relating to rape is but one example of a number of concerted efforts now being made around the United States to deal with the "rape wave." Responding to the "furor" about this crime, the American system of criminal justice is beginning, albeit slowly, to alter long established procedures for investigating and prosecuting forcible rape. In the balance of this chapter, this process of change will be examined primarily by references to data generated by a study conducted by this writer of forcible rape in New York City. The results of this study not only afford an opportunity to comment upon the handling of forcible rape in the largest, single criminal justice unit in the United States but also permit some remarks to be made about the difficulties confronting researchers dealing with official records of crime in a North American setting.[20]

The New York City Study

A total of 704 complaints of forcible rape or attempted rape made to the police in New York City between February 1, 1970, and January 31, 1972, formed the core data source for this study. These 704 complaints represented, approximately, a one in ten random sample of all forcible rapes, and a one in three random sample of all attempted rapes reported to the police in New York City within the two-year period. About 10 percent of the complaints ultimately proved to be unfounded.[21]

The methods adopted to obtain this sample deserve some description for they illustrate the dilemmas facing researchers working with records of a police force as large as that of New York City. To compile a citywide sample in New York City of complaints in any crime category presents significant logistical problems. While the N.Y.P.D. maintains a massive central record bureau for conserving and distributing crime information, it is difficult to tap this data source on a crime-specific basis beyond a precinct level.[b] At the precinct level, and more recently at the divisional level, complaints of crime are kept according to Uniform Crime Report categories as well as in sequential order. But the only synthesis of this data derived from the 75 precincts and 17 divisions of the N.Y.P.D. is a monthly

---

[b]Until July 1971, investigation of rape complaints and almost all other types of crime complaints was the responsibility of precinct-based detectives. Following that date, the detective force of the N.Y.P.D. was involved in a major reorganization with division-based detectives becoming responsible for crime investigations, including rape complaints. The crime record system reflects the organization of the detective force—that is, records being maintained on a crime-specific basis formerly only at the precinct level but now at the divisional level.

crime analysis document prepared by the staff of the department's computer section. This document, in the form of a fifty to sixty pound computer printout, finds its ultimate resting place in the department's Crime Analysis Section.

As might be imagined, monthly crime analysis documents of the weight and magnitude produced in the N.Y.P.D. rapidly come to occupy substantial physical space. The writer discovered that the cramped confines of the N.Y.P.D. Crime Analysis Section permitted the conserving of no more than two years' supply of these documents in dust covered cartons. Each month as a new printout arrived an old one went into the trash.[c] At the time sampling began for this study, the records of February 1970, were the oldest survivors of this cycling process, which thus resulted in the selection of a two-year sampling period from February 1970 through January 1972.

From the monthly computer printouts, the writer identified on a random basis a one in ten sample of all forcible rape complaints and a one in three sample of all atttemped rape complaints. A list of selected complaints was then forwarded to the department's Central Record Section for pulling and copying of specific files. These file copies were subsequently collated by staff members of the Crime Analysis Section. During this collation process, all file references that might permit identification of rape victims were removed. This purging of victim data was one of the conditions imposed upon the writer by the department for gaining access to the rape files.

The destruction of victim data did not ultimately prove to be as debilitating as might have first been anticipated. For when the 704 copied files reached the writer, it was found that in most instances the only victim-related data recorded by the police on a systematic basis—and cut out with scissors from the complaint forms—were complainants' names and addresses. Indeed, not only was there found to be a dearth of information about victims of rape, but the overall quality and quantity of information available concerning all aspects of the reported offenses was, from the researchers' viewpoint, most disappointing.

The N.Y.P.D., like most police forces around the United States, currently uses one type of complaint form (called the U.F. 61) for the initial recording of information about all types of offenses. The file material obtained in the study included a copy of the U.F. 61 completed for each reported offense, together with any additional "Complaint Report: Follow-Up Investigation" sheets attached to the U.F. 61. Follow-up investigation reports are completed by the detectives assigned to the case, while the U.F. 61 is normally filled out by a precinct officer verifying the initial complaint.

The U.F. 61 and allied documents used by the N.Y.P.D.—and most of its law enforcement counterparts throughout America—seem designed to facilitate the

---

[c]It appears that the computer discs used to produce these crimes analysis printouts are not stored in archives, but rather are put back into general circulation. Thus, with the destruction of these printouts, the opportunity to tap detailed citywide historical crime information is irrevocably lost.

gathering of general statistical data about all categories of crime rather than to assist with the task of investigating a particular type of offense, such as forcible rape. A substantial portion of the U.S. 61 is occupied by space to be used for recording details of property stolen in the course of a crime—information rarely relevant in rape. The U.S. 61 may well account in part for the dearth of information recorded by New York City police officers about rape cases. Spot checks made by the writer of U.S. 61s completed for other major crimes, like murder and robbery, indicated that they too were equally devoid of information, however. A relatively uniform style of crime reporting prevailed and was marked by a terseness and tightness of expression as well as legal and police terminology that rarely lapsed into the vernacular. Excerpts drawn from the initial and follow-up reports[d] of two rapes illustrate this point:

Case 1

Details as reported by complainant and/or initial investigating officer: Ptl. R. reports that complainant states that at time and place of occurrence two male P-R [Puerto Rican] did force her into an auto and then in the vicinity of the Brooklyn Bridge did rape her.

Details as reported by follow-up investigating officer:

1. The undersigned interviewed the complainant in this case but she could add no further information than that which she had previously reported.
2. The undersigned interviewed persons in the area of occurrence in an effort to obtain information that would assist in this investigation but this was without results.
3. Alarm No. _____ to remain active.
4. In view of the above stated facts the assigned request that this case be marked CLOSED pending any new developments at which time the prompt and proper POLICE action will be taken.

Case 2

Details as reported by complainant and/or initial investigating officer: Complainant reports to Det. M. that after accepting a ride home from an unknown M/N [Male Negro] he took her to place of occurrence and forcibly raped her.

Details as reported by follow-up investigating officer:

1. Relative to this case, the complainant was personally interviewed by the assigned. The complainant stated that at approximately 1:00 a.m., 4/70, she accepted a ride home from K Street and Broadway, from an unknown male negro who at gunpoint forced her to commit an act of oral sodomy, and at approximately 5:00 a.m. forcibly raped her in the front seat of his auto.
2. Alarm No. _____ transmitted for the perpetrator. On April 11, 1970, the assigned arrested the complainant for P.L. 240-50-3 (FALSE REPORT OF AN INCIDENT) at 7:30 p.m. on the advice of Assistant D.A. after she made statements to him in the presence of the assigned, concerning the incident described above. Statements were also taken by the assigned from an alleged

---

[d]Names of people and other potential identification features have been deleted in these cases. Otherwise the material is reproduced verbatim from the files with no stylistic or other alterations.

suspect, on H., M/N/27, of Brooklyn. In view of the above request that this case be classified as unfounded.

The style and quality of police work reflected by these illustrative cases is strongly reminiscent of that found in the study, mentioned earlier, of police rape files in Boston.[22] In terms applicable to the N.Y.P.D. reports on rape, Boston records are described as being

... notably laconic and vague about the details of what had occurred between the victim and alleged offender. Preliminary moves on the part of each are described, the setting is detailed. Then, according to the typical Boston report, the culprit fell upon his victim and "raped" her! In contrast, the Los Angeles documents tend to be in the nature of Dostoevskian endeavors, with a goodly amount of Mickey Spillane added. The verbal preliminaries of street encounters that end in actual or attempted rape are often detailed word for word. "I'm going to fuck you" is for instance, a routine bit of pre-rape conversation, at least according to the complainants. "This is for you, you God damn whore, you prostitute." "I've heard about you" another offender is quoted as saying. Bras, capris and other garments are often ripped assunder, and the attack on the victim—at least in Los Angeles—is apparently carried on with a fair bit of gusto.[23]

From the researchers' perspective, police reports akin to those found in Los Angeles offer far more substantive data about the generics of rape than do the reports of the Boston and New York police. "The 'officialese' of the Boston [and New York] reports ... carries the impression that the richness of the events has been, perhaps rather summarily, pressed into a pre-ordained formula."[24]

Police records of forcible rape or any other category of crime are not, of course, kept merely to satisfy the research whims of social scientists! They are intended to form the basis of information upon which to initiate an investigation and possible prosecution of a crime as well as to provide documentation of the level of official police activity in any given jurisdiction. Measurement and evaluation of the effectiveness of this activity on a local, regional, or national basis originates from the data contained in police files. Offense incidence and clearance rates are calculated from these official reports to produce the crime statistics presented to the public in the FBI *Uniform Crime Reports*, and elsewhere.

Thus the discovery in New York City of serious data deficiencies in police rape records has implications that extend well beyond the realm of concern of the social scientist. What is in fact missing in many cases from N.Y.P.D. rape files, and the rape files of many other police forces in the United States, is evidence that may be crucial to the successful handling of cases by the prosecution and courts.

Few crimes present such thorny problems for the proper exercise of police discretion as does forcible rape. Rape is not only a crime that is widely unreported but it is also a crime that is often falsely reported. In deciding whether or not a rape complaint is well founded and in ensuring that the necessary elements of the offense are made out, a police officer is called upon to make difficult decisions of law and fact.[25] Often these decisions must be made under conditions of considerable tension and stress, with the officer having to deal with a distraught and incoherent victim. Under the circumstances, it is not surprising an officer who takes the victim's initial complaint may fail to observe, or ask about, very important evidentiary matters. If, as is probably frequently the case, the victim initially reports the crime by phone or personally to an officer having little experience handling rape cases, the chances for evidential clues being missed are increased.

Following the writer's New York study, the development of a new police crime complaint form for reporting rape and allied sexual offenses in New York City is receiving high priority among a number of important changes instituted or planned for the handling of this type of crime. The construction of such a form should aid in preventing clues being missed and assist with the systematic gathering of evidence in rape cases by providing more effective screening data with which to identify at an early stage in an investigation whether or not a complaint is well founded. It is intended that the New York City complaint form should provide a model for adoption by police forces throughout the United States. Other changes, described below, in the handling of rape victims by the N.Y.P.D. are also being viewed with great interest by American criminal justice agencies.[e]

The Treatment of the Rape Victim

Probably no factor is more crucial to the outcome of rape proceedings than the way the victim is treated by the police. Women's groups believe that the present treatment of rape victims by American police represents one of the major deterrents to reporting this crime and to eliciting the further cooperation of those victims who do officially complain that they have been raped. As one rape victim wrote recently:

Why should a woman report a rape to a cop when their typical responses are known to be: "Unless a woman is a virgin, what's the big deal?! Why didn't you just lie back and enjoy it?!!! Tell me the truth: Don't all women secretly want to get raped?"[26]

---

[e]Developments in the rape arena in New York City formed one of the principle topics of discussion at the First National Rape Reduction Workshop sponsored by the Law Enforcement Assistance Administration and held in Denver, Colorado, during May, 1973. These New York City developments are currently being advanced by a large research grant from the Police Foundation. Patrick Murphy, formerly Commissioner of the N.Y.P.D., is now Director of the Foundation.

One of the most sensitive and difficult police tasks in dealing initially with rape victims is eliciting information about the event. The manner in which this information is obtained can have a profound influence on the subsequent attitude adopted by the victim towards the police and the prosecution. In this context, the formation at the beginning of 1972 of the N.Y.P.D. Rape Investigation and Analysis Section represents a most significant advance toward removing the "cold attitude of the sex cops" image.[27] Until the Squad commenced its operations, the role of policewomen in dealing with victims of rape and other sexual attacks in New York City, and probably almost all other police forces in America, was minimal. Reporting on the work assigned policewomen in the N.Y.P.D. as late as 1972, Catherine Milton of the Police Foundation wrote:

... Today more than a third of the policewomen in New York are performing clerical or matron duties. . . . Some 110 (of a total of about 350) policewomen are assigned to patrol precincts. The label is deceptive, however, because the average policewoman does very little patrolling. Most of these policewomen spend the bulk of their time searching female prisoners and dead female bodies, guarding female prisoners, performing clerical duties and running the precinct switchboard. . . . About 65 policewomen are assigned to the Detective Bureau. . . . Some female detectives, like policewomen in other bureaus, are called upon only when someone is needed to play the role of a woman. And some are assigned routine clerical duties. Men are in charge of all the units in the bureau.[28]

With the appointment of a female lieutenant to head the new Rape Squad, men no longer monopolize the command structure of the country's largest detective bureau. The Squad now has the major responsibility for coordinating the investigation of all complaints of rape throughout the N.Y.P.D. This coordination extends to the development of standardized procedures for obtaining a medical examination of the victim; the training of new members of the police force in methods of handling rape cases; the writing of training manuals; and maintaining an effective liaison with the prosecutor's office.

The last named function is one of substantial importance in the American setting. Observations made of rape proceedings in New York City and in other jurisdictions across the country suggest that many rapists evade prosecution simply because of poor liaison between the police, who investigate a rape complaint, and the prosecutor. The first and only contact between staff from these agencies is frequently in the courtroom at the stage of the preliminary hearing. This hearing may often be dealt with by a junior and largely inexperienced assistant district attorney who is working under intense pressure. If any element of the rape case, as presented to him in the court file, appears inadequate or uncertain, it is likely that he will not oppose a motion on the part of defense counsel to dismiss the charge. Insufficient case preparation and specialization, including in particular a lack of prior contact with the victim, can destroy rape prosecutions at the very outset of their course through the court system.

The establishment of a special Rape Squad—like that in New York City—staffed by women can assist greatly in remedying this unsatisfactory situation. Policewomen in a squad of this type are in an excellent position to assist with such essential aspects of case preparation as notifying witnesses promptly of hearing dates and adjournments as well as acting in direct support of the rape victim throughout the ordeal of the prosecution process. If, as in New York City, a female prosecutor is also in charge of rape prosecutions, maximum collaboration is likely between the police and the office of the district attorney.

Jurors and Law Reform

The changes effected or suggested so far for the handling of the current rape problem by the American system of criminal justice have been directed mainly towards the police and prosecution. But it would seem that these changes alone may not be sufficient to produce any marked increase in the conviction rate of rapists in the United States. A vital factor affecting the conviction rate for this crime is the attitude of jurors. As one highly experienced Los Angeles County Prosecutor, offering an explanation of the low conviction rate for rape in his jurisdiction (less than 10 percent) has said:

It [the conviction rate] all depends on the attitudes of the jurors and the cops who handled the rape in the first place. Most of the time, both are inadequate. Jurors are usually 12 hung up people who won't convict in a rape case if they can avoid it. And the police usually don't have the time, manpower or inclination to thoroughly investigate a rape before they dump it on us to prosecute.[29]

Even if the police and prosecution are able to construct a strong case, convincing a jury that a woman has been raped is an exceptionally difficult task. The general cynicism of the male-dominated criminal justice system about rape is apparently shared by jurors:

Unless her head is bashed in or she's 95 years old or it's some other kind of extreme case, jurors just can't believe a woman was raped. There's a suspicion that it was her fault, that she led the guy on, or consented—consent is the hardest thing to disprove. It's just his word against hers.[30]

Given these jury attitudes, reform of the criminal laws relating to rape akin to that described earlier in New York is unlikely to produce any significant alteration in jury behavior. Comparative experience in California already suggests that modification of the corroboration requirements will not, by itself, increase substantially the conviction rate in rape cases nor the deterrent capacity of the criminal justice system.

In California, following the common-law tradition, no special requirements of corroboration are demanded in sexual offenses like rape.[31] In legal theory, California's so-called "non-corroboration" law permits the conviction of an offender on the basis of unsupported testimony of a woman that she was raped. But as the Los Angeles County Prosecutor cited earlier has commented:

Legal theory is not legal reality. . . . And in California, just like anywhere else in this country, a woman who hopes to win a rape case better have plenty of corroboration.[32]

Is there in fact any way in which rape laws might be reformed to make it possible for a woman to win a case without having to be involved in some exceptional circumstances? Certainly the current proposals for law reform circulating among the various American legislatures offer little basis for optimism in this regard. Following the Supreme Court's decision in *Furman v. Georgia*, many states have enacted fresh legislation to re-introduce the death penalty for several well-defined crimes and situations, including in some cases rape.[33] Florida, for instance, has made rape or carnal knowledge of a person under the age of eleven by a person over the age of seventeen a capital felony.[34] Nebraska has reinstated the death penalty for, among other crimes, killing in the course of rape.[35] These and other states, presumably responding to the public's furor rather than reason, have apparently ignored the substantial evidence that indicates conviction rates for crimes tend to decrease when capital punishment is imposed as a penalty.[36] Rather than protecting women against violent sexual attacks, measures of this type seem likely to weaken already vulnerable sanctions. Recognition of this fact is said to have led Governor Thomas Meskill of Connecticut to reject the idea of re-imposing the death penalty for rape in that state.[37] The governor was apparently fearful that the death penalty might cause a rapist to kill his victim rather than risk being identified by her later.

The same furor, which has produced the re-introduction of the death penalty for rape, has also brought with its calls for castration of rapists.[f] Less drastic extralegal remedies suggested by some women's groups have included picketing the residences of suspected rapists and providing lessons in unarmed combat to potential rape victims.

Among all the contemporary discussions and debate about forcible rape, remarkably little attention has been devoted to the proposal advanced by some feminists to "de-escalate" the crime to a form of aggravated assault. Such a "radical" change in the law would, it is argued, alleviate the emotional heat and cultural bias that at present colors any consideration of this crime. Only by

[f]The Reverend Billy Graham apparently was among those favoring this remedy, together with a Baltimore grand jury.

re-definition of the crime, it is said, can our society purge itself of its traditional attitudes and begin to understand and deal with the problem of assaultive sexual behavior upon women and men.

Quite apart from the question of the feasibility of this type of proposal, the possibility appears extremely remote in the present social climate of effecting so major a change to a crime delineated by centuries of tradition. The attitudes that preclude effective prosecution and conviction of rapists are themselves nurtured by this tradition. Modifying these attitudes is likely to be a slow process, and while this process has begun to gather some momentum in the United States, the course to be run remains long and arduous.

Notes

1. R. Brine, *Time*, July 26, 1971, p. 37.

2. An excellent review of the law of rape from a woman's perspective is contained in S. Griffin, "Rape: The All American Crime," *Ramparts Magazine* 10 (1971): 26-35.

3. K. Millett, *Sexual Politics* (New York: Avon Books, Equinox Edition, 1971), p. 44.

4. The plight of rape victims and the male-dominated response of the criminal justice system to the rape problem is ably described by Martha Weinmenn Lear in her article, "Q: If You Rape a Woman and Steal Her T.V., What Can They Get You For in New York? A: Stealing Her T.V.," *New York Times Magazine*, January 30, 1972, p. 11. See also G. Greer, "Seduction is A Four-Lettered Word," *Playboy*, January 1973, p. 80.

5. Eldridge Cleaver, *Soul on Ice* (New York: McGraw Hill, 1968), p. 14.

6. R. Koeninger, "Capital Punishment in Texas," *Crime and Delinquency* 15 (1969): 132-41; D. Partington, "The Incidence of the Death Penalty for Rape in Virginia," *Washington and Lee Law Review* 22 (1965): 43-75.

7. *Furman v. Georgia*, 408 U.S. 238 (1972).

8. Marvin Wolfgang and B. Cohen, *Crime and Race* (New York: Institute of Human Relations, American Jewish Committee, 1970), p. 49. See also M. Agopian, D. Chappell, and G. Geis, "Interracial Rape for a North American City: An Analysis of 66 Cases," paper presented at the American Society of Criminology Conference, Caracas, Venezuela, November, 1972.

9. P. Gray, *Uniform Crime Reporting: 1972 Preliminary Annual Release* (Washington, D.C.: United States Department of Justice, 1973).

10. Ibid., Table 4.

11. President's Commission on Law Enforcement and Administration of Justice, *Task Force Report: An Assessment of Crime and Its Impact* (Washington, D.C.: United States Government Printing Office, 1967), p. 17.

12. B. Kovach, "Study Finds Crime Rates Far Higher Than Reports," *The New York Times*, April 27, 1973.

13. D. Chappell, G. Geis, S. Schafer, and L. Seigel, "Forcible Rape: A Comparative Study of Offenses Known to the Police in Boston and Los Angeles," in J. Henslin, ed., *Studies in the Sociology of Sex* (New York: Appleton-Century Crofts, 1971).

14. Federal Bureau of Investigation, *Uniform Crime Reporting Handbook* (Washington, D.C.: United States Government Printing Office, 1966), p. 17.

15. For a more detailed account of this trend, see D. Chappell, and S. Singer, "Rape in New York City: A Study of Material in Police Files and Its Meaning," *Research Report*, School of Criminal Justice, State University of New York at Albany, March, 1973, pp. 23-25.

16. See, generally, I. Younger, "The Requirements of Corroboration in Prosecutions for Sex Offenses in New York," *Fordham Law Review* 40 (1971): 263-78; and F. Ludwig, "The Case for Repeal of the Sex Corroboration Requirement in New York," *Brooklyn Law Review* 36 (1970): 378-86.

17. Ibid.

18. "An Act to Amend the Penal Law in Relation to Corroboration in Prosecutions for Sex Offenses." [Assembly Bill No. 9203A]. N.Y. Penal Law §130.15 (McKinney Supp. 1972). See also A. Goldstein, "Corroboration in Rape Cases in New York—A Half Step Forward," *Albany Law Review* 37 (1973): 306-28.

19. Executive Committee of the Criminal Justice Co-Ordinating Council, *1972 Criminal Justice Plan* (New York: City of New York, Office of the Mayor, 1972), p. 93.

20. The writer was, in fact, one of the first researchers to seek access to a citywide sample of police records in New York following the announcement in September 1971, of Commissioner Murphy's new "open record" policy for the N.Y.P.D. See "Police Here to Open 'Files and Men' to Academic Researchers," *The New York Times*, September 17, 1971.

21. The New York City level of unfounded complaints is below the United States average. In 1971, the FBI reported that on "a national average, 18 percent of all forcible rapes reported to police were determined by investigation to be unfounded. In other words, the police established that no forcible rape offense or attempt occurred. . . . Crime counts in this publication are limited to actual offenses established by police investigation." P. Gray, *Crime in the United States: Uniform Crime Reports–1971* (Washington, D.C.: U.S. Government Printing Office, 1972), p. 14.

22. Chappell, et al., "Forcible Rape: A Comparative Study of Offenses Known to the Police in Boston and Los Angeles," note 13.

23. Ibid., pp. 182-3.

24. Ibid., p. 183.

25. See "Comment, Police Discretion and the Judgement That A Crime Has Been Committed—Rape in Philadelphia." *University of Pennsylvania Law Review* 117 (1968): 277-321.

26. J. Betries, "Rape: An Act of Possession," *Battle Acts*, April–May, 1972.

27. See "The Rape Wave," *Newsweek*, January 29, 1973, p. 59.

28. C. Milton, *Women in Policing* (Washington, D.C.: Police Foundation, 1972), pp. 73-74.

29. B. Stumbo, "Rape: Does Justice Turn Its Head?" *Los Angeles Times*, March 12, 1972, Section E, p. 1 at p. 9. Copyright 1972, *Los Angeles Times*. Reprinted by Permission.

30. Ibid., pp. 8-9.

31. See Younger, "The Requirements of Corroboration in Prosecutions for Sex Offenses in New York," note 16, p. 264; California Penal Code, Section 261.

32. Stumbo, "Rape: Does Justice Turn Its Head?" note 29, p. 9.

33. The first state to enact a post-*Furman* capital punishment statute was Florida, less than six months after the five-to-four decision was handed down by the Supreme Court. See C. Ehrhardt, and L. Levinson, "Florida's Legislative Response to Furman: An Exercise in Futility?" *Journal of Criminal Law and Criminology* 64 (1973): 10-21.

34. Ibid., p. 17.

35. "Death Penalty in Nebraska," *The New York Times*, April 20, 1973.

36. Schwartz's study of the effect of the increase in penalties for rape in Philadelphia suggests that capital punishment apart, neither the excitement leading up to the imposition of stronger penalties nor the actual imposition of such penalties affected the frequency or seriousness of rape in Philadelphia. B. Schwartz, "The Effect in Philadelphia of Pennsylvania's Increased Penalties for Rape and Attempted Rape," *Journal of Criminal Law, Criminology and Police Science* 59 (1968): 509-15.

37. L. Fellows, "Connecticut Legislature Votes Death Penalty for Sex Crimes," *The New York Times*, April 20, 1973.

8

Gangs, Violence, and Politics

James F. Short, Jr.

In the final report of the National Commission on the Causes and Prevention of Violence—*To Establish Justice, To Promote Domestic Tranquility*—a number of points of special importance for the topic of violence and criminal justice emerged. We called these "Themes of Challenge."

1. As we have noted, not all violence in our society is illegitimate. Indeed, a major function of society is the organization and legitimation of violence in the interest of maintaining society itself. Unfortunately, however, the existence of legitimate violence—from a shooting in lawful self-defense through international violence in the form of warfare—sometimes provides rationalization[a] for those who would achieve ends or express grievances through illegitimate violence.

2. Violence by some individuals may result in part from a deranged mind or abnormal biological make-up. Experts agree, however, that most persons who commit violence—criminal or non-criminal—are basically no different from others, and their behavior is the result of the complex interaction of their biology and life experience. Scholars observe that man has no instinct or trait born within that directs aggression in a specific way. He does have, from birth, the potential for violence. He also has the capacity for creative, constructive activity and for the rejection of violence. Insofar as life experience teaches individuals violence, the incidence of violence is subject to modification, control, and prevention through conscious changes in man's environment.

3. Historically, when groups or individuals have been unable to attain the quality of life to which they believe they are entitled, the resulting discontent and anger have often culminated in violence. Violent protest today—from middle-class students to the inhabitants of the black ghettos and the white ghettos—has occurred in part because the protesters believe that they cannot make their demands felt effectively through normal, approved channels and that "the system," for whatever reasons, has become unresponsive to them.

4. Progress in meeting the demands of those seeking social change does not always reduce the level of violence. It may cause those who feel threatened by change to engage in counter-violence against those seeking to shift the balance. And the pace of change may be slower and more uneven than the challenging group is willing to tolerate. We see these social forces at work in our country today. After several decades of rapid social change, we have better housing, education, medical care, and career opportunities for most groups in our society

---

[a] I much prefer the term "model" to "rationalization," but my phrasing was changed by the Commission in the course of its deliberations. My point was not so much that the types of legitimate violence cited in this paragraph allow people to excuse their own actions, but that the use, and particularly the abuse, of violence by legitimated social control agencies provides important models for those who would engage in violence illegitimately. The Commission recognized that excessive violence by social control agents is itself illegal, but I believe the reliance upon violence by legally constituted authorities has come to be a major problem in our society, and I urge de-escalation of violence wherever possible.

than at any time in the past. Nonetheless, these advances have been uneven, and what we have so far achieved falls short of the needs or expectations of many. Impatience is felt on all sides, and our social order is subject to escalated demand both from those who desire greater stability and from those who desire greater social change.

5. The key to much of the violence in our society seems to lie with the young. Our youth account for an ever-increasing percentage of crime, greater than their increasing percentage of the population. The thrust of much of the group protest and collective violence—on the campus, in the ghettos, in the streets—is provided by our young people. It may be here with tomorrow's generation, that much of the emphasis of our studies and the national response should lie.

6. The existence of a large number of firearms in private hands and a deep-seated tradition of private firearms ownership are complicating factors in the task of social control of violence.

7. Additional complications arise from the high visibility of both violence and social inequalities, resulting from the widespread impact of mass communications media. The powerful impact of the media may aggravate the problems of controlling violence; on the other hand, the media may be one of our most useful social agents for explaining all elements of our society to another and achieving a consensus as to the need for social change that may help to reduce levels of violence.

8. Social control of violence through law depends in large measure on the perceived legitimacy of the law and the society it supports. Persons tend to obey the law when the groups with which they identify disapprove those who violate it. Group attitudes about lawful behavior depend, in turn, on the group's views of the justice provided by the legal order and of the society which created it. The justice and decency of the social order thus are not simply desirable embellishments. On the contrary, a widespread conviction of the essential justice and decency of the social order is an indispensable condition of civil peace in a free society.

With these points in mind we can proceed to the topic of violence within the context, and particularly the political context, of delinquent gangs and their relations with the larger society.

Gangs and Images

The decades of the 1950s and 60s transformed the public image of "delinquent gangs" and of youth generally. "Fighting gangs," romanticized on stage and screen during the 1950s, were overshadowed in the 1960s by assassinations of major public figures, dramatic developments in the civil rights movement, anti-war protests, and riots in most major U.S. cities. The later 1960s saw the emergence of a few "supergangs" whose political and economic activities attracted much attention. More recently, gangs apparently similar to those of the 1950s have again become newsworthy in several major cities.

The thesis I wish to present can be summarized briefly: (1) gangs have changed less than have public images of gangs; (2) the greater accessibility of handguns and the changing ecology of cities have influenced most gang youngsters, individually and collectively, to a greater extent than have recent ideological and political movements; and (3) the politicization of a few gangs in a few cities has occurred primarily as a result of forces external to the gangs rather than from within the established leadership and structure of the gangs.

In the process of these developments, the violence of law enforcement has been fully as important as has the violence of gangs. This includes the violence of the few politicized gangs and of the recently emerged and increasingly significant small terrorist groups. If we would understand these developments and bring them under effective control, it is my considered opinion that the eighth of our "Themes of Challenge" is especially critical. Our fundamental task is to create and maintain "a widespread conviction of the essential justice and decency of the "social order" as the "indispensable condition of civil peace in a free society."

What I am suggesting, then, is that gang life for members of most gangs, individually and collectively, has changed little in recent years, despite impressive publicity to the contrary. Most gang members continue to associate with one another in small groups on countless corners and in other places that identify a turf—their turf—and they can still be found scrimmaging occasionally with one another and with rival gangs, "making out" with girls, vying for status with the limited resources available to them, and otherwise passing the time. There is specialization among some gangs such as, for example, those that have become oriented around narcotics, theft, or reputations as fighting aggregations (Cloward and Ohlin 1960; Short and Strodtbeck 1965). Violence among such groups is a function more of group processes within and between gangs than of ideologically motivated assaults. Violence is more lethal today than a decade or more ago because of the greater availability of handguns that are commercially manufactured, in contrast with the crude, inaccurate, and often misfiring "zip" guns of the 1950s and early 1960s. Horowitz and Schwartz (1974) suggest that the availability of handguns introduces a "zero sum" character to gang conflict that we had not earlier observed in our Chicago research. We argued that most gang fighting was non-zero sum in the sense that most parties to a conflict could take pride in some aspect of violent episodes, even when they were on the losing end (Short and Strodtbeck 1965, Chapter 9). But the change argued by Horowitz and Schwartz apparently is selective. Miller (forthcoming), for example, discusses the far greater use of firearms and therefore the far greater lethality of gang conflict in Philadelphia as compared to Boston in recent years.

The ebb and flow of various drugs has similarly effected the behavior of gang youngsters; some groups have become decimated by drug abuse, while others have participated in the distribution of such substances, and still others have engaged in efforts to drive out the "pushers" of drugs. In some communities, and within some gangs, all three of these activities have occurred in a very confusing picture of inconsistency.

Briefly, with respect to changing ecology, the development of shopping centers and drive-in restaurants as new types of teenage hangouts and the greater mobility of many youngsters as a result of access to automobiles has changed both the ecology of cities and the behavior of young persons in them. These changes are especially significant for cities and rural areas that do not have the gangs found in virtually all very large cities—that is, the *collective processes* associated with delinquency may be very similar in both types of situations, those with and without large-scale gang activity. The specific forms of organization are less important than are the nature of group processes and associated behavior. Little systematic research has been done on these matters, but see Brymmer (1967), Lyman (1972), Miller (forthcoming), and Short (1974a).

Against this background, it is nevertheless the case that a few gangs in a few cities have received a great deal of publicity concerning their "politicization" on the one hand, and on the other, by "going conservative" (engaging in a variety of positive community activities). The impact of these developments has been blown far out of proportion by the resultant publicity, but the implications for poor young people, and especially the black poor, are profound. This chapter surveys these developments against the background of macro- and microsociological processes influencing gangs. Particular attention is focused on the civil rights movement.

The civil rights movement of the 1950s and 1960s exposed young people to a major domestic social problem on an unprecedented scale. Young people often were thrust into the front lines in the struggle of black people for housing, education, and jobs, and for integration of public facilities, both in support of and in militant opposition to the struggle. Black and white youth fought countless battles in cities throughout the country that were undergoing racial transition. Research conducted in Chicago and elsewhere during the late 1950s and early 60s suggests that delinquent gangs often were "innocent" participants in these broad social conflicts, however, and hardly in their vanguard. Even among those gang members drawn into such conflicts, few were affected by the ideological currents of the time, except as those reflected the immediacy of threat perceived by whites to their homes, communities, and institutions.

The primary effect of these movements on gangs was indirect; it was in changing the perceptions and attitudes of others towards gangs and their behavior in relation to them. These effects have been both positive and negative: positive in the sense that government and foundation support has been attracted for legitimate social and economic activities of gangs; negative in that gangs have been perceived as threatening to established economic and political institutions. Combined with the violent and other delinquent activities customarily associated with gang behavior, the effect of the latter has been destructive of "conservative" efforts on the part of some gangs. While precise details are clouded by charges and counter-charges, there is evidence of overreaction on both sides of such conflicts, of naivete concerning the skills and motivations of gang members on the part of their supporters, and vindictiveness and deliberate undermining of gang efforts to achieve respectability on the part of their detractors, notably the police.

In a few instances, powerful institutions and individuals have been polarized over the issue of the "respectability" versus the "criminality" of gangs. The most dramatic illustration of such conflict is the case of the Blackstone Rangers (the Black P. Stone Nation) in Chicago. Here the efforts of foundation and government sponsored programs to utilize the leadership potential of two large gangs for positive economic benefits to a south side Chicago community, and particularly to its young people, was interpreted as a political threat by the city government. A large-scale manpower training program run by gang leadership failed badly amidst charges of fraud and violence by the gangs and harassment by the police (Sherman 1972; Fry 1973; Short 1974b and forthcoming). While a large number of gang and former gang members were affected by these events—and by other attempts to "go conservative" by other gangs—there is little evidence of the success of such efforts, and, to repeat, most gangs in most cities have not been affected by them.

Even among the Stones (Black P. Stone Nation), the degree of political sophistication at the time of their greatest (perceived) threat was questionable. A black politician friend from Chicago, to whom I have talked about the matter, tells me that the most prominent young man among the Stones' leadership was a genius at organization—surely one of the prime desirata for political success—but that his understanding of the political process and that of his fellows among the leadership group was extremely elementary. Shortly after my friend had been elected Alderman of Chicago's 2nd Ward, he was contacted by one of the Stones' leaders who inquired as to "what this politics was all about and how could they [the Stones] get into it." This was at a time when the "political threat" of the Stones was perceived as extremely serious by the city's democratic machine. Asked about their knowledge of how the political system works, and how to make it work, my black politician friend replied that the Stones and other gangs "didn't have it; they don't have it now." He continued, "gangs can play a part, but they can't do it on their own." Such reports of limited political success as are available suggest that this assessment is accurate. Helmreich (1973) describes the Black Crusaders as "a political gang" that enjoyed a brief period of political influence in a large midwestern city. This gang was led by young men in their mid to late twenties, and by a twenty-three year old woman. More commonly, I suspect (regrettably there is little systematic documentation, but see Ianni, forthcoming) that young gang members are more likely to become involved in various forms of organized crime, with its inevitable political ramifications, than in legitimate political activity, whether for lack of opportunity in the political and economic mainstream or as a result of the greater availability (by force and circumstance, certainly not by the generosity or civil rights concerns of entrenched groups involved in organized crime) of less legitimate activities.

Further evidence of the lack of politicization of gangs during the 1960s is offered by reports concerning the nature of gang participation in the ghetto riots in the 1960s. While it is true apparently that an important thrust to black militancy during the 1960s came from high school youth, this thrust did not come from members of delinquent gangs. In a few cases, members of gangs have helped to cool down areas experiencing rioting (Skolnick 1969), and gangs have been involved in massive peaceful demonstrations (which may have been perceived as threatening by established authorities; see Fry 1973). Some have been inclined to interpret these incidents in political terms and as a display of power. Walter Miller's (forthcoming) survey of riot participation by members of gangs strongly suggests, however, that while members of gangs in riot cities usually took part in the rioting, they were not involved in initiating riot activities. As Miller remarks, a riot is almost an ideal situation for the types of activities at which gangs are most adept. But there is little evidence that gangs become politicized in the course of riots or that they played important political roles in the major riots which swept U.S. cities.

Similarly, black militancy has not—until recently—been a major factor in politicization of gangs. The point is made dramatically by Lincoln Keiser in his monograph, "The Vice Lords: Warriors of the Street" (1969). Keiser describes a meeting of the Vice Lords "called to discuss the future of the club" at a time when the Blackstone Rangers had become the most publicized gang in Chicago and hostile incidents with two rival clubs were increasing:

... Bull, who was a member of a militant Black Nationalist organization, had spoken out against a resumption of gang fighting. He felt that all the clubs on the West Side should stop fighting among themselves and unite against the Whites. Others thought that the club's first responsibility was to protect its own members. I was told that, in answer to Bull, another Vice Lord said, "the Cobras may be 'my brothers,' but if one of them fuckers jump on me I'll bust a cap in his ass [shoot him]." The overwhelming number of Vice Lords felt that the group should reorganize to protect themselves and their neighborhoods from hostile clubs, and to reestablish the reputation lost to the Blackstone Rangers. According to my informant, Bull might have been jumped on for his views if he had not left the meeting early (p. 9).

This incident occurred in 1966. Somewhat earlier observations (1959-1962) of the Vice Lords and other gangs my colleagues and I studied are confirmatory. Neither religious (e.g., Black Muslim) nor political (e.g., the Black Panthers) manifestations of Black Nationalism were appealing to these gangs at this time; nor were more traditional political issues and activities. Witness the virtual absence of concern or even discussion among our gangs of the hotly contested presidential election of 1960—an election in which the solidarity of the black ghetto vote for the Democrats proved decisive.[b]

---

[b]For further evidence of the lack of political awareness and concern of the gangs we studied, see Short (1972).

Yet inroads to the gangs clearly were made, as evidenced by the fact that Bull, a Vice Lord leader, "was a member of a militant Black Nationalist organization." Ironically, a Chicago police lieutenant, testifying before the U.S. Senate Permanent Subcommittee on Investigations (the "McClellan Committee" after its chairman) suggested that the failure of the Black Panthers to attract a following among some gangs, notably the Blackstone Rangers and the Disciples, was due to the fact that these gangs were "too well entrenched in the community. They would probably feel that the Black Panther party can offer them nothing. . . ." (Hearings 1969, p. 4446).

The Vice Lords incident cited by Keiser is illustrative of the volatility of the world of fighting gangs—a volatility hardly conducive to stable organization, for political or any other purpose. The world of fighting gangs is an arena where status threats—to individuals (their "rep," their abilities, and in specific roles) and to gangs (*their* "rep," among other gangs and in the public eye, and their turf)—are played out on a day-to-day basis (Short and Strodtbeck 1965).

Politicization of gangs—to the extent that it has occurred—has been the result, primarily of outside and older leadership on the one hand, and of police and other official opposition on the other. The Reverend John Fry, confident and chronicler of the Black P. Stone Nation, suggests that official opposition extended to efforts of the Stones to enter legitimate business enterprise. His description of the "inspection" by city authorities of the premises and facilities in which the Stones planned to open a restaurant at this location is apposite:

The inspector, very tired, almost kindly, said, "Take my word for it, Miss. If you refinish the place in glazed tile and stainless steel and put in brand-new equipment and sterilize the whole thing with Lysol spray every third second, it wouldn't make any different. You—aint—gonna-get-a-license."

Ann thanked him for explaining all of that to them and tried to move the negotiation onto a more positive and informal basis.

"Look," she said, "a restaurant was going on here a week ago, just like you see it now except now there's some new paint on the walls. Everything you see is just like it was then. It didn't run down in a week." She got up from a stool and walked over to the wall. There was a current Board of Health license in a frame. She took it down from the wall and showed it to the inspector. "There is a valid license for this year issued by your department."

The inspector didn't look at the license. He was angry. He had tried to be kind. He said, "I don't have to take your shit." And he walked out.

A detective from the G.I.U. saw some of the guys on 67th Street that night and asked, "When's the restaurant going to open?" and laughed the laugh of the victorious.

It was clear. G.I.U. blocked the restaurant. It is now clear the Stones wanted to have a restaurant, in part, so that G.I.U. detectives would grind their teeth in rage every time they drove by. Beyond that, a restaurant would be an ideal focal point to do business with the peoples going by on the sidewalk. And, it must not be ignored, they might also make "some bread," or cook some (Fry 1973, p. 113).

A former detached worker with the Vice Lords indicates that other community residents were often resentful of private foundation and government programs that appeared to reward gangs that had preyed upon neighborhoods. For some neighborhood residents, this was especially true of the funding of legitimate business. As this ex-detached worker explained, "How is a guy going to feel who has run a business when he sees a bunch of young gang boys without experience getting money to run a competing business? Or if he has had to quit that business because he didn't get that sort of help?"

Large sums were in fact granted gangs for a variety of programs—all quite laudable. Sherman (1972) notes that the Vice Lords (by now the Conservative Vice Lords) in 1968 "received $30,000 in grants from the Rockefeller Foundation and Operation Bootstrap, a grass roots ghetto group. The money went to support a restaurant, an African heritage shop, two recreation centers, a tenants' rights group and a summer beautification project" (p. 22).

A few programs such as these continue to exist, but few have enjoyed much success, and there have been spectacular failures. Though there has been much public concern over the fraudulent use of some of these funds, it is doubtful that any gang members received very much money from such programs, either legitimately or illegitimately. Certainly no gang member ever became even mildly affluent by these means. Even the most sympathetic journalistic accounts of supergang activity have been unable to ignore the severe personal and group problems of gang youngsters seeking to "change their image" by such collective enterprise (Weingarten 1972; Bragonier 1972). Reasons for these failures are not hard to come by, as suggested above. Additionally, it is well to note that small businesses fail by the thousands each year in this country, even when run by knowledgeable adults who are dedicated to their success. There is little reason to believe that gang members possess the required skills and know-how for successful operation of business enterprises. To their lack of technical skills must be added the compounding effects often of their general lack of social skills (Short and Strodtbeck 1965; Klein and Crawford 1967; Gordon 1967). Finally, large-scale organization, if it is to be successful, requires stability, which in turn requires legitimacy. Gang leaders, street-wise and skilled in relations within and between gangs, are not necessarily possessed of large-scale organizational skills—indeed, the transferability of leadership skills in the two situations seems most unlikely. Formal incorporation such as that undertaken by the Conservative Vice Lords in 1967 (as a non-profit organization, claiming 8,000 members in 26 divisions) may look good on paper, but it tells us little about the ability of the organization to carry on its business. The new legal status thus acquired ensures neither the obligation of its members to the organization or the viability of its assets. Legal status does not overcome the social disabilities of many gang youngsters or remove the frequent challenges to leadership and even membership so frequently found in gangs. Hence, legitimacy is likely to be problematic. One of the clearest messages of recent gang literature is the fact that gangs are characteristically unstable as forms of association and organization (see, especially, Short and Strodtbeck 1965).

The extent to which police response to gangs was the result of emerging supergangs, or that the latter were brought into being as a means of gaining protection from police pressure is unknown, and at this point probably unknowable. The expansionist tendencies of gangs has often been noted from the earliest accounts of urban gangs to the present. In any case, the police response in Chicago appears extreme. The Youth Division of the Chicago Police Department was emasculated and a new unit, the Gang Intelligence Unit, a part of the Internal Investigation Division, was created. In the spring of 1969, the G.I.U. was expanded from a force of 38 to 200 men, and "Mayor Daley announced a crackdown on gang violence at a time when gang violence had been declining" (Sherman 1972, p. 23).

. . . Many tactics were used to pursue the goal of destroying the gang leadership. Stirring up intergang conflict was accomplished by spreading rumors and by dropping members of one group deep inside the territory of another group. Another tactic was continual harrassment in the form of miner [sic] traffic violations and stopping gang members on the street for questioning.

In June, 1969, a University of Chicago church group released a report which catalogued the more gruesome G.I.U. attacks on gangs. Although there was little citation of references, the report was never challenged. One of the incidents follows:

Last March (1969) when several rifles were reported stolen from the ROTC unit at Tilden High School, G.I.U. assumed the Rangers had taken them. Mickey Cogwell, a top Ranger leader, was picked up by G.I.U. Officer Stanley Robinson and taken to the lake front at 43rd Street. A known non-swimmer, Cogwell was taken out on the rocks extending into the lake and asked where the guns were. No answer. "Down on your knees, Cogwell." No movement. Robinson beat him to his knees. "Where are the guns?" No answer. The gun fired past Cogwell's head. "We'll give you till 4 o'clock tomorrow to turn over the guns. Then we'll kill you." The guns were later found in the white community. Cogwell has taken a lie detector test verifying his description of the incident.

The tactic of "dropping" members of one group in the territory of another was, of course, especially insidious for it violated the invaded group's conception of "turf." The "dropped" boy often was in great danger, and the practice exacerbated the tensions and threats between gangs that are an ever present feature of gang life.

The police crackdown on gangs was extended to social agencies working with gangs. Youth Action, the umbrella agency in Chicago that brought together the efforts of several agencies working with youth gangs, became a special target. Sherman's description is again apposite:

. . . Youth Action Director Chuck Curry, acknowledging the police image of street workers as "rabble rousers," feels that the hostility was inevitable. "When people are starving," he says, "you can't help stepping on the toes of the political powers, so the soldiers are sicked on you."

Indeed, the soldiers were sicked on Youth Action. On November 19, 1968, the Auburn Center was raided in a weapons hunt, resulting in $250 worth of damage. Four months later three of the policemen involved were suspended. On April 15, 1969, the Woodlawn Youth Action Center was raided with the result of $1,000 damages. Three witnesses gave statements describing the raid but later refused to sign them, allegedly under threats from the police.

In a move to prepare for further incidents, Youth Action executives met in July, 1969, with a volunteer group called Lawyers for a Civil Rights Under Law. The meeting established a procedure for Youth Action staff to have legal services available on a 24 hour basis.

In case of a police incident, a lawyer would go to the scene to gather immediately the relevant information. Staff members were instructed to note such items as badge numbers and squad car numbers.

The intensity of the "war" could not long continue. The Gang Intelligence Unit soon was placed under new leadership and some members were transferred. But much bitterness remained.

The issue raised by this analysis is not whether gangs are responsible for much violence—we know that they are—nor is it a question of whether gang members, individually or collectively, have become involved in organized crime. We know that they have. The issue is why these things have occurred and the question is what will happen in the future. Sherman phrases the issue as follows:

No one doubts that some members of the gang shoot and commit assaults. But the big question about the gang is, do members engage in violence and other crimes because of the gang (as most city officials tend to think) or despite the gang leadership (the view of many youth workers who say the leaders are trying to turn the gang into a militant but legitimate organization). This is an important question, because if the leaders are contributing to delinquency and violence, they belong in jail; if they are trying to snuff out violence to build black community power, they deserve help.

We can conclude at least that the reasons for gang involvement in violence and crime are not attributable solely to the members of gangs but involve in important ways the reactions of others, notably the police and their superiors in political power. I am skeptical of the ability of gangs to lead in the quest for legitimate political and economic power, for the reasons suggested in this chapter. The basis for my skepticism lies also in fundamental structural constraints on the ability of poor people in our society to manage their problems without far greater economic and technical assistance than has been invested even in the celebrated "War on Poverty." In the final analysis, such constraints and the unwillingness of the larger society to make necessary changes and to accommodate legitimate aspirations seem likely to force black people, especially, toward organized crime as a basis for economic progress. The black politician to whom I referred earlier in this chapter puts it this way:

Black people ain't never going to make it until they can get it all together. . . . Blacks have a chance right here [in Chicago]. . . . The jails are full of blacks, and here they have a black warden, a black deputy warden and blacks in other top jobs. . . . Blacks will make it only when these guys get out of jails and take over organized crime. I think politics will put it all together—business, jobs, crime, power. Some people think it will be economic, but that ain't going to happen until we get it all together, and that will be through politics.

Given our present economic system and the forces and processes described in this chapter, this analysis is at least a viable hypothesis. The additional threat posed by emerging terrorist groups in our society and the politicization of large numbers of minority groups in prisons and jails throughout the country (Jacobs 1974) suggest that time may be growing short for us to meet these problems on a more realistic basis. Here we are confronted basically with two alternatives. We can either react with repression, in which case the violence and terror may in the long run destroy any semblance of the society of freedom and equality to which we aspire, or we can react by addressing more fundamentally than we have ever been willing to do the basic causes of social unrest. I hope we will have the wisdom to adopt the latter strategy, but I am not optimistic.

References

Bragonier, R. 1972. "The 'Prez' of the Reapers: A New Style City Street Gang." *Life Magazine*, August 25.

Brymmer, R.A. 1967. "Toward a Definition and Theory of Conflict Gangs." Paper delivered at annual meeting of Society for the Study of Social Problems, August 26, mimeographed.

Cloward, Richard A. and Lloyd E. Ohlin. 1960. *Delinquency and Opportunity: Theory of Delinquent Gangs.* New York: Free Press of Glencoe.

Fry, John. 1973. *Locked-Out Americans.* New York: Harper and Row.

Gordon, Robert A. 1967. "Social Level, Disability, and Gang Interaction." *American Journal of Sociology* 73:42-62.

Helmreich, William B. 1973. "Black Crusaders." *Society* 11:44-50.

Horowitz, Ruth and Gary Schwartz. 1974. "Honor, Normative Ambiguity and Gang Violence." *American Sociological Review* 39.

Ianni, Francis A.J. 1974. "Black Mafia: Ethnic Succession in Organized Crime." New York: Simon Schuster.

Jacobs, James B. 1974. "Street Gangs Behind Bars." *Social Problems* 21:395-409.

Keiser, R. Lincoln. 1969. *The Vice Lords: Warriors of the Streets.* New York: Holt, Rinehart & Winston.

Klein, M.W. and L.Y. Crawford. 1967. "Groups, Gangs and Cohesiveness." *Journal of Research in Crime and Delinquency* 4:63-75.

Lyman, Scott R. 1972. "Participant Observer Analysis of an Adolescent Subculture," unpublished.

Miller, Walter B. Forthcoming. "American Youth Gangs: Past and Present." In Abraham S. Blumberg, ed., *Current Issues in Criminology* New York: Alfred A. Knopf.

National Commission on the Causes and Prevention of Violence. 1969. *To Establish Justice, To Insure Domestic Tranquility: Final Report.* Washington, D.C.: U.S. Government Printing Office.

Sherman, Lawrence W. 1970. "Youth Workers, Police and the Gangs: Chicago, 1956-1970." Unpublished Master's Thesis, University of Chicago.

_____. 1972. "Street Work History Includes Three Stages." *The Journal of the Association of Professional Directors of YMCA's in the United States* (May):17-24. Reprinted by permission.

Short, James F., Jr. 1972. "Gangs, Politics and the Social Order." Paper read at the Symposium in Delinquency Studies in honor of Henry D. McKay. University of Chicago. To be published in the symposium volume.

_____. 1974a. "Collective Behavior, Crime and Delinquency." In Daniel Glaser, ed., *Handbook of Criminology*. Chicago: Rand-McNally.

_____. 1974b. "Youth, Gangs and Society: Micro and Macro-Sociological Processes." *The Sociological Quarterly* (February):3-19.

Short, James F., Jr. and F.L. Strodtbeck. 1965. *Group Process and Gang Delinquency*. Chicago: University of Chicago Press.

Skolnick, Jerome. 1969. "The Politics of Protest." Report of the Task Force on Demonstrations, Protests, and Group Violence, National Commission on the Causes and Prevention of Violence. Washington, D.C.: U.S. Government Printing Office.

United States Senate Permanent Subcommittee on Investigations 1969. Hearings.

Weingarten, Gene. 1972. "East Bronx Story—Return of the Street Gangs." *New Yorker* (March 27):31-7.

Violence and Criminal Justice: A Bibliography, 1969-1974

Faith Fogarty

Introduction

Increasing worldwide concern and preoccupation with the causes and effects of violence is very much in evidence judging by the abundance of material written and published on the subject. The explosive sixties precipitated masses of research and literature on violence that reached a pinnacle in the definitive and voluminous reports of the National Commission on the Causes and Prevention of Violence in 1969.[a] The purpose of this bibliography is to gather together a selective list of materials published on violence since the National Commission's reports—that is, from 1969 through late 1974.

The subject of violence is multifaceted and, likewise, the literature on violence falls into several general categories that have been used as headings to divide this bibliography into sections. Naturally, there are overlappings and interrelations among the different categories, so it is advisable to check more than one section of this listing when seeking references to any particular aspect of violence. The titles of these sections are as follows:

General Perspectives on Violence,
Collective and System Violence,
Psychological Aspects of Violence,
Sexual Violence,
The Mass Media and Violence,
Juvenile Violence,
Child Abuse and Violence in the Family,

[a]National Commission on the Causes and Prevention of Violence, Task Force Reports, 13 Volumes (Washington, D.C.: U.S. Government Printing Office, 1969):

Violence in America: Historical and Comparative Perspective, Volumes I and II;
The Politics of Interest: Violent Aspects of Protest and Confrontation, Volume III;
Rights in Concord: The Response to the Counter-Inaugural Protest Activities in Washington, D.C., Volume IV;
Shoot-Out in Cleveland: Black Militants and the Police, Volume V;
Shut It Down!: A College in Crisis, Volume VI;
Firearms and Violence in American Life, Volume VII;
Assassination and Political Violence, Volume VIII;
Mass Media and Violence, Volume IX;
Law and Order Reconsidered, Volume X;
Crimes of Violence, Volumes XI-XIII;
To Establish Justice, To Insure Domestic Tranquility, Final Report.

Drug-Induced Violence,
Compensation to Victims of Violent Crimes.

General Perspectives on Violence

This broad category covers a variety of works on the subject of violence that are
mainly sociological and ideological. Many of these works are concerned with
what is referred to in one case as the "crisis of violence" in America—that is,
general attitudes and values, combined with a tradition and a system, that have
produced a climate where violence is almost normative. Literature on general
theories of violence and on violence in other cultures is included in this section.

Abrahamsen, D. 1970. *Our Violent Society*. New York: Funk and Wagnalls.
Abudu, M.J.G. 1972. "American Black Ghetto Revolt: A New Perspective."
Police Journal 45:13-25.
Aiken, H.D. 1972. "Violence and the Two Liberalisms." *Social Theory and
Practice* 2:47-66.
Apple, R.W. 1970. "Reflections on Violence." *New Statesman* 80:262.
Arendt, H. 1970. *On Violence*. New York: Harcourt, Brace & Jovanovich.
Aromaa, K. 1971. *Arkipäivän väkivaltaa suomessa* [*Everyday Violence in
Finland—A Survey*]. Series M:11. Helsinki: Institute of Criminology.
Ball-Rokeach, S.J. 1973. "Values and Violence: A Test of the Subculture of
Violence Thesis." *American Sociological Review* 38:736-749.
Bardis, P.D. 1973. "Violence: Theory and Quantification." *Journal of Political
and Military Sociology* 1:121-46.
Barnett, A. and Kleitman, D.J. 1973. "Urban Violence and Risk to the
Individual." *Journal of Research in Crime and Delinquency* 10:111-6.
"Bekämpfung der Gewaltkriminalität" ["Controlling Crimes of Violence"].
1971. *Die Neue Polizei* 25:177-8. Munich.
Berkowitz, L. and Macaulay, J. 1971. "The Contagion of Criminal Violence."
Sociometry 34:238-60.
Bingham, J.B. and Bingham, A.M. 1970. *Violence and Democracy*. New York:
World Publishing Co.
Block, I. 1970. *Violence in America*. New York Public Affairs pamphlet, no.
450. New York: Public Affairs Committee.
Blumenthal, M.D. 1973. "Resentment and Suspicion among American Men."
American Journal of Psychiatry 130:876-80.
Blumenthal, M.D., Kahn, R.L., Andrews, F.M., and Head, K.B. 1972. *Justifying
Violence: Attitudes of American Men*. Ann Arbor: Institute of Social
Research, University of Michigan.
Bondurant, J.V. 1971. *Conflict: Violence and Non-Violence*. Chicago: Aldine-
Atherton.

115

Boydell, C.L. and Grindstaff, C.F. 1974. "Public Opinion Toward Legal Sanctions for Crimes of Violence." *Journal of Criminal Law and Criminology* 65:113-6.

Brown, R.M. 1970. *American Violence.* Englewood, N.J.: Prentice-Hall.

Cameron, J.M. 1973. "Changing Patterns of Violence." *Medicine, Science, and the Law* 13:261-4. London.

Coates, J.F. 1973. "Urban Violence: Pattern of Disorder." *Annals of the American Academy of Political and Social Science* 405:25-40.

Cormier, B.M. 1971. "Violence: Individual and Collective Aspects." *Criminology* 9:99-116.

Council of Europe. 1973. *Violence in Society. Tenth Congress of Directors of Criminal Research Institutes, Strasbourg, 28 November-1 December 1972.* Strasbourg: Council of Europe.

Critchley, T.A. 1970. *The Conquest of Violence: Order and Liberty in Britain.* London: Constable.

Daniels, D.N., Gilula, M.F., and Ochberg, F.M. 1970. *Violence and the Struggle of Existence.* Boston: Little, Brown & Co.

Demaris, O. 1970. *America the Violent.* New York: Cowles Book Co.

Dotson, A.B. 1974. "Social Planning and Urban Violence: An Extension of McElroy and Singell." *Urban Affairs Quarterly* 9:283-301.

Dworkin, A.G., ed. 1971. "Symposium on Violent Confrontation." *Sociological Quarterly* 12:291-406.

Edwards, G.R. 1972. *Jesus and the Politics of Violence.* New York: Harper & Row.

Erskine, H. 1974. "Polls: Fear of Violence and Crime," *Public Opinion Quarterly* 38:131-45.

Estey, G.F. and Hunter, D.A. 1971. *Violence: A Reader in the Ethics of Actions.* Lexington, Mass.: Xerox College Publishing Co.

Faulkner, R.K. 1973. "Respect and Retribution: Toward an Ethnography of Violence." *Sociological Symposium,* no. 9, 17-35.

Fawcett, J., ed. 1972. *Dynamics of Violence.* Chicago: American Medical Association.

Ferracuti, F., Lazzari, R., and Wolfgang, M., eds. 1970. *Violence in Sardinia.* Rome: Mario Bulzone Editore.

Fraser, J. 1974. *Violence in the Arts.* Cambridge, England: Cambridge University Press.

Gastil, R.D. 1971. "Homicide and a Regional Culture of Violence." *American Sociological Review* 36:412-27.

Gert, B. 1969. "Justifying Violence." *Journal of Philosophy* 66:616-28.

Gibbens, T.C.N. 1970. "How Should We Treat Violent Offenders?" *New Society* 16:408-10. London.

Gould, J.A. and Iorio, J.J. 1972. *Violence in Modern Literature.* San Francisco: Boyd and Fraser Publishing Co.

Graham, H.D., Mahinka, S., and Rudoy, D.W., eds. 1971. *Violence: The Crisis of American Confidence.* Baltimore: Johns Hopkins Press.

Gray, J.G. 1970. *On Understanding Violence Philosophically, and Other Essays.* New York: Harper & Row.

Greenwood, C. 1973. "Controlling Violent Crime." *New Society* 24:491-3. London.

Grundy, K.W. and Weinstein, M.A. 1974. *Ideologies of Violence.* Columbus, Ohio: C.E. Merrill Publishing Co.

Gunn, J. 1973. *Violence.* New York: Praeger Press.

Harries, K.D. 1973. "Spatial Aspects of Violence and Metropolitan Population." *Professional Geography* 25:1-6.

Harris, J. 1974. "The Marxist Conception of Violence." *Philosophy and Public Affairs* 3:192-220.

Harris, P. 1973. "The Concept of Violence." *Political Science* 25:103-13.

Hepburn, J.R. 1971. "Subcultures, Violence and the Subculture of Violence: An Old Rut or a New Road?" *Criminology* 9:87-98.

Hofstadter, R. and Wallace, M., eds. 1970. *American Violence: A Documentary History.* New York: Alfred Knopf.

Hollon, E. 1974. *Frontier Violence: Another Look.* New York: Oxford University Press.

Hook, S. 1970. "Ideology of Violence." *Encounter* 34:26-29.

————. 1973. "Myth and Fact in the Marxist Theory of Revolution and Violence." *Journal of the History of Ideas* 34:271-80.

Iglitzin, L.B. 1970. "Violence and American Democracy." *Journal of Social Issues* 26:165-86.

————. 1972. *Violent Conflict in American Society.* San Francisco: Chandler Publishing Co.

Johnston, S.W. 1971. "The Violence of the Continued Claim to National Sovereignty Today." *Australian and New Zealand Journal of Criminology* 4:132-43. Melbourne.

Jones, K.M. 1971. *Bibliography on Personal Violence: An Index for Understanding and Prevention, 1950-1971.* Sponsored by the Moody Foundation. Houston: Texas University.

Kahn, R.L. 1972a. "The Justification of Violence: Social Problems and Social Solutions." *Journal of Social Issues* 28:155-75.

————. 1972b. "Violent Man: Who Buys Bloodshed and Why." *Psychology Today* 6:47-48, 82-84.

Katz, M. 1974. "Violence and Civility in a Suburban Milieu." *Journal of Police Science and Administration* 2:239-49.

Kiefer, T.M. 1972. *The Tausug: Violence and Law in a Philippine Moslem Society.* New York: Holt, Rinehart & Winston.

Klein, M.M. 1973. "The Face Of Violence in America: An Historical Perspective." *Social Education* 37:540-5.

Knopf, T.A. 1970. "Sniping: A New Pattern of Violence?" *Reflections* 5:13-30.

Kreps, G.A. and Weller, J.M. 1973. "The Police-Community Relations Movement: Conciliatory Responses to Violence." *American Behavioral Scientist* 16:402-12.

Laqueur, W. 1972. "Reflection on Violence." *Encounter* 38:3-10.

Lawrence, J. 1970. "Violence." *Social Theory and Practice* 1:31-49.

Lewis, J.U. 1971. "Law in the Schools: Violence in the Streets." *Canadian Bar Association Journal* 2:10-12.

Lincoln, A.J. 1973. "Justifications and Condemnations of Violence: A Typology of Responses and a Research Review." *Sociological Symposium*, no. 9, 51-67.

Liston, R.A. 1974. *Violence in America: A Search for Perspective.* New York: Julian Messner.

Mark, R. 1971. "Social Violence." *Criminologist* 6:5-14.

Maybanks, E.F. 1972. "Police View of Violence and the Control of Violence." *Medicine, Science, and the Law* 12:262-5. London.

Menninger, W.W. 1970. "Violence and the Urban Crisis." *Crime and Delinquency* 16:229-37.

_____. 1971a. "The Psychiatrist and the Violence Commission." *American Journal of Psychiatry* 128:431-6.

_____. 1971b. "Violence Commission and Corrections: An Update." *American Journal of Correction* 33:22-26.

Moran, R. 1971. "Criminal Homicide: External Restraint and Subculture of Violence." *Criminology* 8:357-74.

Murphy, J.G. 1970. "Violence and the Rule of Law." *Ethics* 80:319-21.

Nahrendorf, R.O. 1971. "Violence and Social Change." *Sociology and Social Research* 56:5-18.

Nash, J. 1973. "The Cost of Violence." *Journal of Black Studies* 4:153-83.

Nieburg, H.L. 1973. *Culture Storm: Politics and the Ritual Order.* New York: St. Martin's Press.

Normandeau, A. 1972. "Violence and Robbery." *Acta Criminologica* 5:11-106. Montreal.

Paddock, J. and Genoves, S. 1974. "Violence and Behavior. Symposium on the Origins of Man's Inhumanity to Man." *American Journal of Physical Anthropology* 41:1-5.

Payne, E.A. 1971. "Violence, Non-Violence and Human Rights." *The Ecumenical Review* 23:222-36.

Perry, C. 1970. "Violence: Visible and Invisible." *Ethics* 81:1-21.

Pinkney, A. 1973. "Aggression, Violence and American Character." *American Journal of Orthopsychiatry* 43:287.

_____. 1972. *The American Way of Violence.* New York: Random House.

Prosterman, R.L. 1972. *Surviving to 3000: An Introduction to the Study of Lethal Conflict.* Belmont, Calif.: Duxbury Press.

Ranly, E.W. 1972. "Defining Violence." *Thought* 47:415-27.

Rittberger, V. 1973. "International Organization and Violence with Special Reference to the Performance of the United Nations System." *Journal of Peace Research*, no. 3, 217-26. Oslo.

Romanucci-Ross, L. 1973. *Conflict, Violence, and Morality in a Mexican Village.* Palo Alto: National Press Books.

Rose, T., ed. 1969. *Violence in America: A Historical and Contemporary Reader.* New York: Random House.

Schaff, A. 1973. "Marxist Theory on Revolution and Violence." *Journal of the History of Ideas* 34:263-70.

Schumacher, M. 1971. *Violent Offending. A Report on Recent Trends in Violent Offending and Some Characteristics of the Violent Offender.* Wellington, N.Z.: New Zealand Justice Department.

Shaffer, J.A., ed. 1971. *Violence: Award-Winning Essays in the Council for Philosophical Studies Competition.* New York: D. McKay Co.

Shapiro, H. 1972. "Afro-American Responses to Race Violence during Reconstruction." *Science and Society* 36:158-70.

Sheppard, C. 1971. "The Violent Offender: Let's Examine the Taboo." *Federal Probation* 35:12-19.

Simpson, E. 1970. "Social Norms and Aberrations: Violence and Some Related Social Facts." *Ethics* 81:22-35.

Sitkoff, H. 1971. "Racial Militancy and Interracial Violence in the Second World War." *Journal of American History* 58:661-81.

Sloan, I.J. 1970. *Our Violent Past: An American Chronicle.* New York: Random House.

Stevens, H.S. 1972. "Violence and the Law." *New York State Journal of Medicine* 72:2157-9.

Stott, L. 1972. "Values and Violence." *Educational Theory* 22:403-10.

Sugg, C., ed. 1970. *Violence.* New York: Paulist/Newman Press.

Takaki, R. 1972. *Violence in the Black Imagination; Essays and Documents.* New York: G.P. Putnam's Sons.

Taylor, K.K. and Soady, F.W. 1972. *Violence: An Element of American Life.* Boston: Holbrook Press.

Tignor, R.L. 1972. "Maasai Warriors: Pattern Maintenance and Violence in Colonial Kenya." *Journal of African History* 13:271-90.

Toch, H. 1970. "Change Through Participation (and Vice Versa)." *Journal of Research in Crime and Delinquency* 7:198-206.

Vigh, J., Gönczöl, K., Kiss, G., and Szabo, A. 1973. *Eröszakos Büncselekmények és Elkövestöik [Violent Crimes].* Budapest: Közgazdasági és Könyukiadó.

"Violence against Nurses." 1972. *British Medical Journal* 4:129-30. London.

Wade, F.C. 1971. "On Violence." *Journal of Philosophy* 68:369-77.

Westley, W.A. 1970. *Violence and the Police: A Sociological Study of Law, Custom and Morality.* Cambridge, Mass.: M.I.T. Press.

Whitlock, F.A. 1971. *Death on the Road: A Study in Social Violence.* London: Tavistock Publishing Ltd.

Wiener, P.P. and Fisher, J. 1974. *Violence and Aggression in the History of Ideas.* New Brunswick, N.J.: Rutgers University Press.

Williams, E.B. 1971. "Crime, Punishment, Violence: The Crisis in Law Enforcement." *Judicature* 54:418-23.

Williams, J.E. 1972. "Treatment of Violence." *Medicine, Science, and the Law* 12:269-74. London.

Zevin, J., ed. 1973. *Violence in America: What is the Alternative?* Englewood Cliffs, N.J.: Prentice-Hall.

Collective and System Violence

"Violence has been pursued in the defense of order by the satisfied, in the name of justice by the oppressed, and in fear of displacement by the threatened." This quote from the final report of the National Commission on the Causes and Prevention of Violence, *To Establish Justice, To Insure Domestic Tranquility* (Washington, D.C.: U.S. Government Printing Office, 1969, p. 57) aptly sums up the subject matter of most of the references listed in this section of the bibliography. Both collective (insurrectionary or mob) violence and system (official or sanctioned) violence are considered under one heading because much of the literature dealing with one concerns the other. This is logical, since one form often occurs in reaction to the other. Violence by groups—from terrorism to police riots—used to obtain political and social ends makes up a good proportion of recent literature on violence.

Abudu, M.J.G. et al. 1972. "Black Ghetto Violence: A Case Study Inquiry into the Spatial Pattern of Four Los Angeles Riot Event-Types." *Social Problems* 19:408-26.

Abu-Lughod, I. 1973. "Unconventional Violence and International Politics." *American Journal of International Law* 67:100-111.

Adamek, R.J. and Lewis, J.M. 1973. "Social Control Violence and Radicalization: The Kent State Case." *Social Forces* 51:342-7.

Adams, J.P. 1973. "Kent State: Justice and Morality." *Cleveland State Law Review* 22:26-47.

"Anatomy of a Riot." 1972. *New Society* 21:336-7. London.

Arendt, H. 1972. *Crisis of the Republic: Lying in Politics, Civil Disobedience, on Violence, Thoughts on Politics and Revolution.* New York: Harcourt, Brace & Jovanovich.

Aya, R. and Miller, N., eds. 1970, *Revolution Reconsidered.* New York: Free Press.

Backman, E.L. and Finlay, D.J. 1973. "Student Protest: a Cross-National Study." *Youth Society* 5:3-46.

Becker, H.K. 1972: "The Danish Police and Violence." *Journal of Criminal Law, Criminology and Police Science* 63:444-6.

Bell, J.B. 1972. "Chroniclers of Violence in Northern Ireland: The First Wave Interpreted." *Review of Politics* 34:147-57.

Blake, J.A. 1970. "The Organization as an Instrument of Violence: The Military Case." *Sociological Quarterly* 11:331-50.

Brady, D. and Rappoport, L. 1973. "Violence and Vietnam: Comparison between Attitudes of Civilians and Veterans." *Human Relations* 26:735-52.

Causes, Preventive Measures, and Methods of Controlling Riots and Disturbances in Correctional Institutions. 1970. Washington, D.C.: American Corrections Association.

Civil Violence and the International System. 1971. London: International Institute for Strategic Studies.

Clutterback, R.L. 1973. *Protest and the Urban Guerrilla.* London: Cassell.

Conant, R.W. 1971. *The Prospects for Revolution: A Study of Riots, Civil Disobedience, and Insurrection in Contemporary America.* New York: Harper's Magazine Press.

Cosier, L.A. et al. 1972. "Collective Violence and Civil Conflict." *Journal of Social Issues* 28:1-212. (See entire issue.)

Craig, G.A. and Paret, P. 1972. "The Control of International Violence: Historical Notes." *Stanford Journal of International Studies* 7:1-21.

Cromwell, P.E. and Lewis, R.L. 1971. "Crowds, Mobs, and Riots: A Sociological Analysis." *Police* 16:30-32.

Cross, M.S. 1973. "The Shiners' War: Social Violence in the Ottawa Valley in the 1830s." *Canadian Historical Review* 54:1-26.

Davis, N.Z. 1973. "The Rites of Violence: Religious Riot in 16th Century France." *Past and Present*, no. 59, 51-91.

Drew, P. 1974. "Domestic Political Violence: Some Problems of Measurement." *Sociological Review* 22:5-25.

Edelman, J.B. 1971. *Politics as Symbolic Action: Mass Arousal and Quiescence.* Chicago: Markham Publishing Co.

Elliot-Bateman, M., ed. 1970. *The Fourth Dimension of Warfare.* New York: Praeger Press.

Ellis, D. 1973. *Violence in Prisons.* Lexington, Mass.: Lexington Books.

Ellis, D., Grasmick, H.G., and Gilman, B. 1974. "Violence in Prisons: A Sociological Analysis." *American Journal of Sociology* 80:16-43.

Feagin, J.R. and Hahn, H. 1973. *Ghetto Revolts: The Politics of Violence in American Cities.* New York: Macmillan.

Feierabend, I.K., Feierabend, R.L., and Nesvold, B.A. 1973. "A Comparative Study of Revolution and Violence." *Comparative Politics* 5:393-424.

Firestone, J.M. 1972. "Theory of the Riot Process." *American Behavioral Scientist* 15:859-82.

Fogelson, R.M. 1970. "Violence and Grievances: Reflections on the 1960s Riots." *Journal of Social Issues* 26:141-63.

Fogelson, R.M. 1971. *Violence as Protest: A Study of Riots and Ghettos.* Garden City, N.Y.: Doubleday.

Fogelson, R.M. and Rubenstein, R., selectors. 1970. *Mass Violence in America. A Collection of 43 Books Revealing America's Collective Aggression from Pre-Revolutionary Days to the Present.* New York: Arno Press.

Forman, E.M. 1972. "Civil War as a Source of International Violence." *Journal of Politics* 34:1111-34.

Fox, V. 1972. "Prison Riots in a Democratic Society." *Police* 16:35-41.

Friedrich, C.J. 1972. "Opposition, and Government, by Violence." *Government and Opposition* 7:3-19.

_____. 1972. *The Pathology of Politics: Violence, Betrayal, Corruption, Secrecy, and Propaganda.* New York: Harper & Row.

Gallemore, J.L., Jr. 1972. "Observations during Post-Riot Convalescence in a State Prison." *Corrective Psychiatry and Journal of Social Therapy* 18:21-25.

Gamson, W.A. 1974. "Violence and Political Power: The Meek Don't Make It." *Psychology Today* 8:35.

Gamson, W.A. and McElvoy, J. 1972. "Police Violence and Its Public Support." In J. Susman, ed., *Crime and Justice, 1970-1971: An AMS Anthology.* New York: AMS Press.

Garson, G.D. 1972. "Force Versus Restraint in Prison Riots." *Crime and Delinquency* 18:411-21.

Goode, W.J. 1972. "Presidential Address: The Place of Force in Human Society." *American Sociological Review* 37:507-19.

Gross, F. 1972. *Violence in Politics: Terror and Political Assassination in Eastern Europe and Russia.* The Hague: Mouton.

Gude, E.W. 1973. "Dealing with Worldwide Terror." *Society* 10:9, 11.

Gurr, T.R. 1972. "The Calculus of Civil Conflict." *Journal of Social Issues* 28:27-47.

_____. 1970. *Why Men Rebel.* Princeton, N.J.: Princeton University Press.

Hahn, H.D. 1970. "Civil Responses to Riots: A Reappraisal of Kerner Commission Data." *Public Opinion Quarterly* 34:101-7.

Halaby, C.N. 1973. "Hardship and Collective Violence in France: A Comment." *American Sociological Review* 38:494-501.

Hendel, S., ed. 1971. *The Politics of Confrontation.* New York: Appleton-Century-Crofts.

Hibbs, D.A., Jr. 1973. *Mass Political Violence: A Cross-National Causal Analysis.* New York: John Wiley and Sons.

Hindus, M. 1971. "A City of Mobocrats and Tyrants: Mob Violence in Boston 1747-1863." *Issues in Criminology* 6:55-83.

Hirsch, H. and Perry, D.C. 1973. *Violence as Politics: A Series of Original Essays.* New York: Harper and Row.

Honderich, T. 1973. "Democratic Violence." *Philosophy and Public Affairs* 2:190-214.

Hoover, J.E. 1970. "Law Enforcement Faces the Revolutionary Guerrilla Criminal." *F.B.I. Law Enforcement Bulletin* 39:20-22, 28.

Horowitz, I.L. 1970. *The Struggle is the Message: The Organization and Ideology of the Anti-War Movement.* Berkeley, Calif.: Glendessary Press.

Horowitz, R. and Schwartz, G. 1974. "Honor, Normative Ambiguity and Gang Violence," *American Sociological Review* 39:238-51.

Hudson, M.C. 1970. *Conditions of Political Violence and Instability: A Preliminary of Three Hypotheses.* Beverly Hills, Calif.: Sage Publications.

Hutchinson, M.C. 1972. "The Concept of Revolutionary Terrorism." *Journal of Conflict Resolution* 16:383-96.

Leeke, W.D. 1971. "Collective Violence in Correction Institutions." *American Journal of Correction* 33:12-16.

Lodhi, A.Q. and Tilly, C. 1973. "Urbanization, Crime, and Collective Violence in 19th-Century France." *American Journal of Sociology* 79:296-318.

Marsh, J.J. 1973. "Operations Analysis and Corrections." *American Journal of Correction* 35:24-28.

Martinson, R. 1972. "Collective Behavior at Attica." *Federal Probation* 36:3-7.

Mattick, H.W. 1973. "The Prosaic Sources of Prison Violence." *Australian and New Zealand Journal of Criminology* 6:12-20. Melbourne. Also in *Public Welfare* 31:54-60.

Miller, L. 1972. "Identity and Violence: In Pursuit of the Causes of War and Organized Violence." *Israel Annals of Psychiatry and Related Disciplines* 10:71-77. Jerusalem.

Mitra, S.K. 1971. "Group Aggression and Research on Violence." *International Social Science Journal* 23:98-103.

Momboisse, R.M. 1970. *Riots, Revolts and Insurrections.* Springfield, Ill.: C.C. Thomas.

Moreno, F.J. and Mitrani, B., eds. 1971. *Conflict and Violence in Latin American Politics: A Book of Readings.* New York: T.Y. Crowell.

Muller, E.N. 1972. "Test of a Partial Theory of Potential for Political Violence." *American Political Science Review* 66:928-59.

Nardin, T. 1971. *Violence and the State: A Critique of Empirical Political Theory.* Beverly Hills, Calif.: Sage Publications.

New York State Special Commission on Attica. 1972. *Attica: Official Report.* New York: Bantam Books.

Opton, E.M. 1974. "Psychiatric Violence Against Prisoners: When Therapy is Punishment." *Mississippi Law Journal* 45:605-44.

Platt, A.M. 1971. *The Politics of Riot Commissions 1917-1970: A Collection of Official Reports and Critical Essays.* New York: Collier Books.

Rosenbaum, H.J. and Sederberg, P.C. 1974. "Vigilantism: An Analysis of Establishment Violence." *Comparative Politics* 6:541-70.

Rosenthal, C.F. 1971. *Social Conflict and Collective Violence in American Institutions of Higher Learning.* Vol. I: *Dynamics of Student Protest*; Vol. II: *Bibliography.* Kensington, Md.: American Institutes for Research.

Rossi, P.H., ed. 1970. *Ghetto Revolts.* New Brunswick, N.J.: Transactions Books.

Rubenstein, R.E. 1970. *Rebels in Eden: Mass Political Violence in the United States.* Boston: Little, Brown & Co.

Sanford, N. and Comstock, C. 1971. *Sanctions for Evil: Sources of Social Destructiveness.* San Francisco: Jossey-Bass, Inc.

Sears, D.O. and McConahay, J.B. 1970. "Racial Socialization, Comparison Levels, and the Watts Riot." *Journal of Social Issues* 26:121-40.

Short, J.F. and Wolfgang, M.E. 1972. *Collective Violence.* Chicago: Aldine-Atherton.

Singer, B.D., Osborn, R.W., and Geschwender, J.A. 1970. *Black Rioters: A Study of Social Factors and Communications in the Detroit Riot.* Lexington, Mass.: D.C. Heath and Co.

Spackman, A. 1973. "Official Attitudes and Official Violence: The Ruimveldt Massacre, Guyana, 1924." *Social and Economic Studies* 22:315-34.

Stark, R. 1972. *Police Riots: Collective Violence and Law Enforcement.* Belmont, Calif.: Wadsworth Publishing Co.

Swomley, J.M., Jr. 1972. *Liberation Ethics.* New York: Macmillan.

Terrell, L.M. 1972. "Patterns of International Involvement and International Violence." *International Studies Quarterly* 16:167-86.

U.S. Congress. Select Committee on Crime. 1972. *American Prisons in Turmoil,* Part I: Hearings held November 29, 30, December 1, 2, 3, 1971; Part II: Hearings held February 12 and June 15, 1972. Washington, D.C.: U.S. Government Printing Office.

U.S. President's Commission on Campus Unrest. 1970. *Report.* Washington, D.C.: U.S. Government Printing Office.

U.S. Senate. Judiciary Committee. 1970. *Assaults on Law Enforcement Officers; Hearings.* Washington, D.C.: U.S. Government Printing Office.

Van den Haag, E. 1972. *Political Violence and Civil Disobedience.* New York: Harper & Row.

Van den Muijzenberg, O.D. 1973. "Political Mobilization and Violence in Central Luzon (Philippines)." *Modern Asian Studies* 7:691-705.

Vestermark, S.D., Jr. 1971. *Responses to Collective Violence in Threat or Act,* Vol. I: *Collective Violence in Educational Institutions*; Vol. II: *Collective Violence in Actions by Extremist Groups.* McLean, Va.: Human Sciences Research.

Von der Mehden, F.R. 1973. *Comparative Political Violence.* Englewood Cliffs, N.J.: Prentice-Hall.

Wagner, F. and Cohen, F., eds. 1971. "Attica: A Look at the Causes and the Future." *Criminal Law Bulletin* 7:817-43.

Wells, A. 1973. "Mass Violence in India since 1960." *Indian Political Science Review* 7:125-130.

Wells, D.A. 1970. "Is 'Just Violence' Like 'Just War'?" *Social Theory and Practice* 1:26-38.

White, A.G. 1973. *Organized Violence in Urban Areas: A Selected Bibliography.* Monticello, Ill.: Council of Planning Libraries.

Wolfe, A. 1973. *The Seamy Side of Democracy: Repression in America.* New York: D. McKay Co.

Psychological Aspects of Violence

The literature referred to in this section mainly concerns the psychodynamics of violence and aggressive behavior. Personality types and psychological determinants of violence are the major subjects discussed in these works, along with the question of whether violence can be predicted or prevented.

Abrahamsen, D. 1973. *The Murdering Mind.* New York: Harper & Row.

Bach-y-Rita, G. and Veno, A. 1974. "Habitual Violence: A Profile of 62 Men." *American Journal of Psychiatry* 131:1015-7.

Bauer, G. 1971. "Gewalttätige Triebverbrecher. Eine Analyse ihrer Entwicklung und ihres Verhaltens" ["Violent Impulsive Offenders. An Analysis of Their Development and Behavior"]. *Münchener Medizinische Wochenschrift* 113:1089-96. Munich.

Berkowitz, L. 1970. "Experimental Investigations of Hostility Catharsis." *Journal of Consulting and Clinical Psychology* 35:1-7.

Berlin, A. 1972. "Treatment for the Violent Offender." *Crime and Delinquency Literature* 4:101-15.

Bey, D.R. and Zecchinelli, V.A. 1974. "G.I.'s Against Themselves: Factors Resulting in Explosive Violence in Vietnam." *Psychiatry* 37:221-8.

Blumenthal, M.D. 1972. "Predicting Attitudes toward Violence." *Science* 176:1296-303.

Bogaards, C. and Steenstra, S.J. 1972. "Agressie en geweld: een psychologische beschouwing" ["Aggression and Violence: A Psychological Discussion"]. *Nederlands Tijdschrift voor de Criminologie* 14:156-74. Meppell, Netherlands.

Briggs, D.L. 1972. "A Traditional Therapeutic Community for Young, Violent Offenders [in the California Institution for Men, Chino]." *Howard Journal of Penology and Crime Prevention* 13:171-84. London.

Bylinsky, G. 1973. "New Clues to the Causes of Violence." *Fortune* 87:134.

Climent, C.E., Rollins, A., Ervin, F.R., and Plutchik, R. 1973. "Epidemiological Studies of Women Prisoners: Medical and Psychiatric Variables Related to Violent Behavior." *American Journal of Psychiatry* 130:985-90.

Cocozza, J.J. and Steadman, H.J. 1974. "Some Refinements in the Measurement and Prediction of Dangerous Behavior." *American Journal of Psychiatry* 131:1012-4.

Davies, J.C. 1970. "Violence and Aggression: Innate or Not?" *Western Political Quarterly* 23:611-23.

Delgado, J.M.R. 1971. "The Neurological Basis of Violence." *International Social Science Journal* 23:27-35.

125

Dercole, K.L. and Davenport, W.G. 1974. "Social Psychophysics: Measurement of Attitudes toward Violence." *Perceptual and Motor Skills* 38:135-45.

Ellenberger, H.F. 1971. "Violence et Dangérosité" ["Violence and Dangerousness"]. *Annales Internationales de Criminologie* 10:345-52. Paris.

Evseeff, G.S. and Wisniewski, E.M. 1972. "A Psychiatric Study of a Violent Mass Murderer." *Journal of Forensic Sciences* 17:371-6.

Ferracuti, F. and Wolfgang, M.E. 1973. *Psychological Testing of the Subculture of Violence.* Rome: Bulzoni Editore.

Frank, J.D. 1972. "Some Psychological Determinants of Violence and its Control." *Australian and New Zealand Journal of Psychiatry* 6:158-64. Carlton.

Fromm, E. 1973. *The Anatomy of Human Destructiveness.* New York: Holt, Rinehart & Winston.

Geen, R.G. and Stonner, D. 1974. "The Meaning of Observed Violence: Effects on Arousal and Aggressive Behavior." *Journal of Research in Personality* 8:55-63.

Genthner, R.W. and Taylor, S.P. 1973. "Physical Aggression as a Function of Racial Prejudice and the Race of the Target." *Journal of Personality and Social Psychology* 27:207-10.

Greenland, C. 1971. "Violence and Dangerous Behavior Associated with Mental Illness: Prospects for Prevention." *Canadian Journal of Criminology and Corrections* 13:331-9.

Häfner, H. and Böker, W. 1973. "Mentally Disordered Violent Offenders." *Social Psychiatry* 8:220-9.

Hartocollis, P. 1972. "Aggressive Behavior and the Fear of Violence." *Adolescence* 7:479-90.

Hildreth, A.M.N., Derogatis, L.R., and McCusker, K. 1971. "Body Buffer Zone and Violence: A Reassessment and Confirmation." *American Journal of Psychiatry* 127:1641-5.

Johnson, R.N. 1972. *Aggression in Man and Animals.* Philadelphia: W.B. Saunders.

Jones, K. 1974. "Violence and the Mentally Handicapped." *New Society* 27:247-9. London.

Justice, B., Justice, R., and Kraft, I.A. 1974. "Early-Warning Signs of Violence: Is a Triad Enough?" *American Journal of Psychiatry* 131:457-9.

Lidberg, L. 1971. "Frequency of Concussion and Type of Criminality: A Preliminary Report." *Acta Psychiatrica Scandinavica* 47:452-61. Copenhagen.

Lion, J.R. and Pasternak, S.A. 1973. "Countertransference Reactions to Violent Patients." *American Journal of Psychiatry* 130:207-10.

Lyons, H.A. 1973. "Violence in Belfast: A Review of the Psychological Effects." *Community Health* 5:163-8. Also in *Public Health* 87:231-8.

Mantell, D.M. 1971. "The Potential for Violence in Germany." *Journal of Social Issues* 27:101-12.

Maple, T. and Matheson, D.W., eds. 1973. *Aggression, Hostility, and Violence: Nature or Nurture?* New York: Holt, Rinehart & Winston.

Mark, V.H. and Ervin, F.R. 1970. *Violence and the Brain.* New York: Harper & Row.

May, R. 1972. *Power and Innocence: A Search for the Sources of Violence.* New York, Norton.

Meerloo, J.A.M. 1970. "Eichmannism: Cold Violence and Robotized Pugnacity." *Psychoanalytic Review* 56:609-14.

Megargee, E.I. and Hokanson, J.E. 1970. *The Dynamics of Aggression: Individual, Group, International Analyses.* New York: Harper & Row.

Möllhoff, G. 1972. "Unerkannte paranoide Entwicklungen als Ursachen von Gewaltverbrechen. Ein Beitrag aus forensisch-psychiatrischer Sicht" ["Unrecognized Paranoid Developments as Causes of Aggressive Crime. A Forensic-Psychiatric View"]. *Archiv für Kriminologie* 149:129-43. Lübeck.

Moyer, K.E. 1973. "The Physiology of Violence." *Psychology Today* 7:35.

Nicol, A.R., Gunn, J.C., Foggitt, R.H., and Gristwood, J. 1972. "Quantitative Assessment of Violence in Adult and Young Offenders." *Medicine, Science, and the Law* 12:275-82. London.

Nordlicht, S. 1972. "Determinants of Violence." *New York State Journal of Medicine* 72:2163-5.

Parker, R.S., ed. 1972. *The Emotional Stress of War, Violence, and Peace.* Pittsburgh: Stanwix House.

Petzel, T.P. and Michaels, E.J. 1973. "Perception of Violence as a Function of Levels of Hostility." *Journal of Consulting and Clinical Psychology* 41:35-36.

Roth, M. 1972. "Human Violence as Viewed from the Psychiatric Clinic." *American Journal of Psychiatry* 128:1043-56.

Scharff, W.H. and Schlottmann, R.S. 1973. "Effects of Verbal Reports of Violence on Aggression." *Journal of Psychology* 84:283-90.

Schwartz, M.M. 1973. "The 'Use of Force' and the Dilemma of Violence." *Psychoanalytic Review* 59:617-25.

Sheppard, C. 1971. "Toward a Better Understanding of the Violent Offender." *Canadian Journal of Criminology and Corrections* 13:60-67.

Singer, J.L., ed. 1971. *The Control of Aggression and Violence: Cognitive and Physiological Factors.* New York: Academic Press.

Spiegel, J.P. 1972. "The Dynamics of Violent Confrontation." *International Journal of Psychiatry* 10:93-108.

Tardiff, K.J. 1974. "A Survey of Psychiatrists in Boston and Their Work with Violent Patients." *American Journal of Psychiatry* 131:1008-11.

Teoh, J.-I. 1972. "The Changing Psychopathology of Amok." *Psychiatry* 35:345-51.

Toch, H. 1969. *Violent Men: An Enquiry into the Psychology of Violence.* Chicago: Aldine Publishing Co.

Usdin, G., ed. 1972. *Perspectives on Violence.* New York: Bruhner-Mazel, Inc.

Virkkune, M. 1974. "Observations on Violence in Schizophrenia." *Acta Psychiatrica Scandinavica* 50:145-51. Copenhagen.

Warder, J. 1969. "Two Studies of Violent Offenders: I: Neurosis and Character Disorder in Violent Offenders; II: Personality Variables in Violent Offenders." *British Journal of Criminology* 9:389-93.

Wenk, E.A., Robinson, J.O., and Smith, G.W. 1972. "Can Violence Be Predicted?" *Crime and Delinquency* 18:393-402.

Westermeyer, J. 1973. "Epidemicity of Amok Violence." *Archives of General Psychiatry* 28:873-6.

Wilkins, J.L., Scharff, W.H., and Schlottmann, R.S. 1974. "Personality Type, Reports of Violence and Aggressive Behavior." *Journal of Personality and Social Psychology* 30:243-7.

Sexual Violence

The amount of literature[b] on sexual violence has increased rapidly in the past decade, as has the occurrence of this type of violence itself, and is concentrated mainly in the subject areas of forcible rape, dangerous sex offenders, and homosexual assault, primarily in prisons.

Forcible rape has become a particularly publicized and much written about subject due to a combination of factors: the startling increase in the number of (reported) rapes in recent years; the feminist movement's espousal of rape as one of its major concerns; and the socio-psychological dynamics of rape that have interested social scientists for the implications this phenomenon has on the general social and psychic conditions of our society.

Agopian, M.W., Chappell, D., and Geis, G. 1974. "Interracial Forcible Rape in a North American City: An Analysis of Sixty-Three Cases." In I. Drapkin and E. Viano, eds., *Victimology*. Lexington, Mass.: Lexington Books.

Amir, M. 1971a. "Forcible Rape." *Sexual Behavior* 1:25-36.

_____. 1971b. *Patterns in Forcible Rape.* Chicago: University of Chicago Press.

Bauer, G. 1970. "Triebverbrecher jugendlicher und minderjähriger Delinquenten" ["Sex Crimes by Juvenile Delinquents"]. *Praxis der Kinderpsychologie und Kinderpsychiatrie* 19:234-7. Göttingen.

_____. 1971. "Gewalttätige Triebverbrecher. Eine Analyse ihrer Entwicklung und ihres Verhaltens" ["Violent Impulsive Offenders: An Analysis of Their Development and Behavior"]. *Münchener Medizinische Wochenschrift* 113:1089-96. Munich.

Bertschmann, E. 1970. "Zum Sexualproblem in Unseren Strafanstalten Strafan-

[b]N.B.: A recently published bibliography on forcible rape is available and contains many more references on that subject than can be cited here. The bibliography has over 300 citations and should be consulted for further references; see Chappell, D., Geis, G., and Fogarty, F., "Forcible Rape: Bibliography," cited in this section.

stalt Basel-Stadt" ["Sexual Problems in Our Penal Institutions"]. *Zeitschrift für Strafvollzug* 19:158-67. Wiesbaden.

Brittain, R.P. 1970. "The Sadistic Murderer." *Medicine, Science, and the Law* 10:198-207. London.

Chappell, D., Geis, G., and Fogarty, F. 1974. "Forcible Rape: Bibliography." *Journal of Criminal Law and Criminology* 65:248-63.

Chatz, T.C. 1972. "Recognizing and Treating Dangerous Sex Offenders." *International Journal of Offender Therapy and Comparative Criminology* 16:109-15. London.

Clinch, N.G. and Schurr, C. 1973. "Rape." *Washingtonian Magazine* 8:86.

Cohen, M.L., Garofalo, R., Boucher, R., and Seghorn, T. 1971. "The Psychology of Rapists." *Seminars in Psychiatry* 3:307-27.

Davis, A.J. 1970. "Sexual Assaults in the Philadelphia Prison System." In J.H. Gagnon and W. Simon, eds. *The Sexual Scene.* Chicago: Aldine.

Geis, G. and Chappell, D. 1971. "Forcible Rape by Multiple Offenders." *Abstracts on Criminology and Penology* 11:431-6.

Gilder, G.F., 1973. *Sexual Suicide.* New York: Quadrangle.

Goldner, N.S. 1972. "Rape as a Heinous but Understudied Offense." *Journal of Criminal Law, Criminology and Police Science* 63:402-7.

Goldstein, M., Kant, H., Judd, L., Rice, C., and Green, R. 1971. "Experience with Pornography: Rapists, Pedophiles, Homosexuals, Transsexuals, and Controls." *Archives of Sexual Behavior* 1:1-15.

Greenland, C. 1972. "Dangerous Sex Offenders in Canada." *Canadian Journal of Criminology and Corrections* 14:44-54.

Griffin, S. 1971. "Rape: The All-American Crime." *Ramparts* 10:26-35.

Hayman, C.R. and Lanza, C. 1971. "Sexual Assault on Women and Girls." *American Journal of Obstetrics and Gynecology* 109:480-6.

Hayman, C.R., Lanza, C., Fuentes, R., and Algor, K. 1972. "Rape in the District of Columbia." *American Journal of Obstetrics and Gynecology* 113:91-97.

Hopper, C.B. 1971. "Sexual Adjustment in Prisons." *Police* 15:75-76.

Howell, L.M. 1972-1973. "Clinical and Research Impressions Regarding Murder and Sexually Perverse Crimes." *Psychotherapy and Psychosomatics* 21:156-9.

Johnson, E. 1971. "The Homosexual in Prison." *Social Theory and Practice* 1:83-95.

MacDonald, J.M. 1971. *Rape Offenders and Their Victims.* Springfield, Ill.: C.C. Thomas.

Mintz, B. 1973. "Patterns in Forcible Rape: A Review-Essay." *Criminal Law Bulletin* 9:703-10.

National League of Cities—U.S. Conference of Mayors. 1974. *Rape.* A monograph on rape in Denver and the Denver Rape Reduction Project. Washington, D.C., April, 1974.

Richmond, R.G.E. 1970. "The Homosexual in Prison." *Canadian Journal of Corrections* 12:553-5.

Rooth, G. 1973. "Exhibitionism, Sexual Violence and Paedophilia." *British Journal of Psychiatry* 122:705-10. London.

Roth, L.H. 1971. "Territoriality and Homosexuality in a Male Prison Population." *American Journal of Orthopsychiatry* 41:510-3.

Schiff, A.R. 1973a. "Rape in Foreign Countries." *Medical Trial Technique Quarterly* 20:66-74.

_____. 1973b. "A Statistical Evaluation of Rape." *Forensic Science* 2:339-49.

Schulman, G.I. 1974. "Race, Sex, and Violence: A Laboratory Test of the Sexual Threat of the Black Male Hypothesis." *American Journal of Sociology* 79:1260-77.

"Sexual Assaults and Forced Homosexual Relations in Prison: Cruel and Unusual Punishment." 1972. *Albany Law Review* 36:428-38.

Shaffer, H.B. 1972. "Crime of Rape." *Editorial Research Reports*, January 19, 43-60.

The Mass Media and Violence

Although most public concern has been focused on the possible detrimental effects of violence portrayed in the mass media on members of society, particularly impressionable youth, there are, on the other hand, those who feel that violence presented in the media could and does have a cathartic effect on the aggressive tendencies of humans. Others would discount any effect media violence had on any human behavior. The national government (DHEW) joined the debate and published a five-volume report on the effects of television on social behavior in 1972 (see U.S. Department of Health, Education and Welfare, this section).

All sides of the media-violence controversy—both here and abroad—are represented in the publications listed in this section.

Alloway, L. 1971. *Violent America: The Movies, 1946-1964.* New York: Museum of Modern Art.

Anderson, J.A. 1972. "Television and Growing Up: The Impact of Televised Violence." *Journal of Broadcasting* 16:224-7.

Artus, H.H. 1970. " ' . . . jedenfalls schwerstens jugend gefährdend'—über die Wirkung brutaler Filme" [" ' . . . in any case very harmful to the young'—on the Effect of Violent Films"] . *Jugendschutz* 15:172-6. Darmstadt.

Beaugrand, G. 1971. "Das Speil mit der Gewalt" ["Playing with Violence"] . *Jugendwohl* 52:377-8. Freiburg.

_____. 1972. "Das Klischee der Gewalt. Psychologische Dauer Wirkungen von Kriminalsendungen auf dem Bildschirm" ["The Stereotype of Violence. Lasting Psychological Effects of Television Crime Films"], *Jugendwohl* 53:277-8. Freiburg.

Berkowitz, L. 1971. "Sex and Violence: We Can't Have It Both Ways." *Psychology Today* 5:14,18-23.

Berkowitz, L., Parke, R.D., Leyens, J.P., and West, S.G. 1974. "Reactions of Juvenile Delinquests to Justified and Less Justified Movie Violence." *Journal of Research in Crime and Delinquency* 11:16-24.

Bogart, L. 1973. "Warning: The Surgeon General Has Determined that TV Violence is Moderately Dangerous to Your Child's Mental Health." *Public Opinion Quarterly* 36:491-521.

British Broadcasting Corporation. 1972. *Violence on Television: Program Content and Viewer Perception; A BBC Audience Research Department Report.* New York: International Publications Service.

Burnet, M. 1971. *Mass Media in a Violent World.* Paris: UNESCO.

Carruthers, M. and Taggart, P. 1973. "Vagotonicity of Violence: Biochemical and Cardiac Responses to Violent Films and Television Programmes." *British Medical Journal* 3:384-9. London.

Carruthers, M., Taggart, P., and Somerville, W. 1973. "The Heart's Response to the Portrayal of Violence." *Medicine, Science, and the Law* 13:252-5. London.

Cline, V.B., Croft, R.G., and Courrier, S. 1973. "The Desensitization of Children to Television Violence." *Journal of Personality and Social Psychology* 27:360-5.

Coffin, T.E. and Tuchman, S. 1973. "Rating Television Programs for Violence: A Comparison of Five Surveys." *Journal of Broadcasting* 17:3-20.

Drabman, R.S. and Thomas, M.H. 1974. "Does Media Violence Increase Children's Toleration of Real-Life Aggression?" *Developmental Psychology* 10:418-21.

Dussich, J.P.J. 1970. "Violence and the Media." *Criminology* 8:80-94.

Eleey, M.F., Gerbner, G., and Tedesco, N. 1973. "Apples, Oranges, and the Kitchen Sink: An Analysis and Guide to Comparison of Violence Ratings." *Journal of Broadcasting* 17:21-31.

Emmett, B.P. 1973. "The Presentation of Violence on TV." *Medicine, Science, and the Law* 13:256-60. London.

Feshbach, S. and Singer, R.D. 1971. *Television and Aggression: An Experimental Field Study.* San Francisco: Jossey-Bass.

Fyrel, T.R. 1970. "Children of the Television Age." *Encounter* 35:46-52.

Glucksmann, A. 1971. *Violence on the Screen: A Report on Research into the Effects on Young People of Scenes of Violence in Films and Television.* Translated from French by Susan Bennet. London: British Film Institute, Education Department.

Hagenauer, F. and Hamilton, J.W. 1973. "Straw Dogs: Aggression and Violence in Modern Film." *American Imago* 30:221-48.

Haskins, J.B. 1973. "The Cloud-with-a-Silver-Lining Approach to Violence News." *Journalism Quarterly* 50:549-52.

Heller, M.S. and Polsky, S. 1971. "Television Violence: Guidelines for Evaluation." *Archives of General Psychiatry* 24:279-85.

Holper, J.J., Goldstein, J.H., and Snyderman, P. 1973. "The Placement of Neutral Stimulus Material in Reducing the Effects of Mass Media Violence on Aggression." *Representative Research in Social Psychology* 4:28-35.

Howitt, D. and Dembo, R. 1974. "A Subcultural Account of Media Effects." *Human Relations* 27:25-41.

Johnson, P.H. et al. 1970. "Peddling the Pornography of Violence." *Encounter* 34:70-76; 34:85-90; 35:64-70; 35:84-87; 35:95-96.

Knopf, T.A. 1970. "Media Myths on Violence." *New Society* 16:856-9. London.

Krebs, D. 1973. "Wirkungen von Gewaltdarstellungen in Massenmedien—Katharsis oder Stimulation" ["Effects of Violence in the Mass Media: Catharsis or Stimulation"]. *Zeitschrift für Sozialpsychologie* 4:318-32. Frankfort.

Lang, G.E. and Lank, K. 1972. "Some Pertinent Questions on Collective Violence and the News Media." *Journal of Social Issues* 28:93-110.

Lichty, L.W. and Bailey, G.A. 1972. "Violence in Television News: A Case Study of Audience Response." *Central States Speech Journal* 23:225-9.

Liebert, R.M. and Baron, R.A. 1972. "Some Immediate Effects of Televised Violence on Children's Behavior." *Developmental Psychiatry* 6:469-75.

Liebert, R.M., Neale, J.M., and Davidson, E.S. 1973. *The Early Window: Effects of Television on Children and Youth.* New York: Pergamon.

"Looking at Violence." 1973. *British Medical Journal* 2:565-6. London.

Meyer, T.P. and Anderson, J.A. 1973. "Media Violence Research: Interpreting the Findings," *Journal of Broadcasting* 17:447-58.

Murray, J.P. 1973. "Television and Violence: Implications of the Surgeon General's Research Program." *American Psychologist* 28:472-8.

Pinderhughes, C.A. 1972. "Televised Violence and Social Behavior." *Psychiatric Opinion* 9:28-36.

Rein, D.M. 1974. "The Impact of Television Violence." *Journal of Popular Culture* 7:934-45.

Roshier, R.J. 1972. "Media Violence and Deviancy." *Criminologist* 7:65-71. London.

Rubenstein, E.A. 1974. "TV Violence Report: What's Next?" *Journal of Communication* 24:80-88.

Shaw, C. and Baker, R. 1972. "Violence on Television." *Medicine, Science, and Law* 12:248-56.

Snow, R.P. 1974. "How Children Interpret TV Violence in Play Context." *Journalism Quarterly* 51:13-21.

Tudor, A. 1973. "Screen Violence." *New Society* 25:154-5. London.

U.S. Department of Health, Education and Welfare. National Institute of Mental Health. 1971. *Television and Social Behavior: Annotated Bibliography on Research Focusing on Television's Impact on Children.* Edited by C.K. Atkin, J.P. Murray, and O.B. Nayman. Public Health Service Publication No. 2099. Washington, D.C.: U.S. Government Printing Office.

U.S. Department of Health, Education and Welfare. National Institute of Mental Health. 1972. *Television and Social Behavior*. Technical Reports to the Surgeon General's Scientific Advisory Committee on Television and Social Behavior, 5 Volumes. DHEW Publication No. HSM 72-9059. Washington, D.C.: U.S. Government Printing Office.

Wotring, C.E. and Greenberg, B.S. 1973. "Experiments in Televised Violence and Verbal Aggression: Two Exploratory Studies." *Journal of Communication* 23:446-60.

Juvenile Violence

Many of the references in the preceding section (Mass Media and Violence) dealing with the effects of televised and filmed violence on youth are also relevant to this section of the bibliography, which contains studies on violence in youth. Research and theories on motivating factors behind juvenile violence make up the majority of these works.

Adams, K.A. 1974. "The Child Who Murders: A Review of Theory and Research." *Criminal Justice and Behavior* 1:51-61.

Adelson, L. 1972. "The Battering Child." *Journal of the American Medical Association* 222:159-61.

"Adolescent Violence." 1973. *New Society* 26:664-5. London.

Andrew, J.M. 1974. "Violent Crime Indices Among Community-Retained Delinquents." *Criminal Justice and Behavior* 1:123-30.

Cohen, S. 1971. "Direction for Research on Adolescent Group Violence and Vandalism." *British Journal of Criminology* 11:319-40. London.

_____. 1973. "Some Sociological Problems in the Study of Adolescent Violence." *Proceedings of the Royal Society of Medicine* 66:1131-2. London.

Feshbach, S. and Feshbach, N. 1973. "The Young Aggressors." *Psychology Today* 6:90-95.

Foster, H.L. 1971. "To Reduce Violence: The Intervenist Teacher and Aid." *Phi Delta Kappan* 53:59-62.

Hahn, P.H. 1971. *The Juvenile Offender and the Law*. Cincinnati: W.H. Anderson.

Littner, N. 1972. "Violence as a Symptom of Childhood Emotional Illness." *Child Welfare* 51:208-19.

Marchandise, T. 1973. "L'Aggressivité et la Protection Morale de las Juenesse" ["Aggressiveness and the Moral Protection of the Young"]. *Revue de Droit Pénale et de Criminologie* 53:957-71. Brussels.

Meyer, T.P. 1973a. "Children's Perceptions of Justified/Unjustified and Fictional/Real Film Violence." *Journal of Broadcasting* 17:321-32.

"More Muscle in the Fight to Stop Violence in Schools." 1973. *U.S. News and World Report* 74:113-6.

Patch, R.K. 1974. "Enuresis, Fire Setting and Male Adolescent Delinquents: A Triad Predictive of Violent Behavior." *Journal of Psychiatry and Law* 2:45-72.

Perry, D.G. and Perry, L.C. 1974. "Denial of Suffering in the Victim as a Stimulus to Violence in Aggressive Boys." *Child Development* 45:55-62.

Rawlings, M.L. 1973. "Self-Control and Interpersonal Violence: A Study of Scottish Adolescent Male Severe Offenders." *Criminology* 11:23-45.

Robert, P., Pasturaud, C., Krementchousky, A., and Lambert, T. 1970. "Jeunes Adultes Délinquants. Les Viols Collectifs" ["Young Adult Delinquents. Group Rape"]. *Annales Internationales de Criminologie* 9:657-82. Paris.

Russell, D.H. 1973. "Juvenile Murderers." *International Journal of Offender Therapy and Comparative Criminology* 17:235-9. London.

Russell, J. 1973. "Violence and the Ulster Schoolboy." *New Society* 25:204-6. London.

Seijas Candelas, L.R. 1972. "Los Origenes de la Violencia Juvenil" ["The Origins of Juvenile Violence"]. *Policía Espanola* 11:43-44. Madrid.

Soukop, J.F. 1973. "Torture Toys, Parental Rights and the First Amendment." *Southern California Law Review* 46:184-201.

Wenk, F.A. and Emrich, R.L. 1972. "The Assaultive Youth: An Exploratory Study of the Assaultive Experience and Assaultive Potential of California Youth Authority Wards." *Journal of Research in Crime and Delinquency* 9:171-96.

Wolfgang, M.E. 1970. *Youth and Violence.* DHEW publication. Washington, D.C.: U.S. Government Printing Office.

Zimbardo, P.G. 1970. *A Social-Psychological Analysis of Vandalism: Making Sense out of Senseless Violence.* A technical report. Stanford: University of California, Department of Psychology, December.

Child Abuse and Violence
in the Family

In the literature on violence published during the last four years, child abuse (also known as "the battered child syndrome") has not been neglected. The problem is a serious but delicate one and only fairly recently have states begun enacting law making it mandatory for certain people to report known cases of child abuse.

What sort of people are baby batterers? How extensive is the physical and mental damage done to the battered child? What is or can be done to combat this tragic form of violence? These are the questions addressed in the literature listed in this section. Also included here is the subject of violence amongst family members, which is related to child abuse and is equally difficult to manage.

Bakan, D. 1972. *Slaughter of the Innocents. A Study of the Battered Child Phenomenon.* Boston: Beacon Press.

"Battered Babies." 1970. *Lancet* 2:1248.

Bean, S.L. 1971. "The Parents' Center Project: A Multiservice Approach to the Prevention of Child Abuse." *Child Welfare* 50:277-82.

Blumberg, M.L. 1974. "Psychopathology of the Abusing Parent." *American Journal of Psychotherapy* 28:21-29.

Boisvert, M.J. 1972. "The Battered-Child Syndrome." *Social Casework* 53:475-80.

Burland, J.A., Andrews, R.G., and Headsten, S. 1973. "Child Abuse: One Tree in the Forest." *Child Welfare* 52:588-92.

DeCourcy, P. and DeCourcy, J. 1973. *A Silent Tragedy: Child Abuse in the Community.* Port Washington, N.Y.: Alfred Publishing Co.

"Deliberate Injury of Children." 1973. *British Medical Journal* 4:61-62. London.

Diggle, G. and Jackson, G. 1973. "Child Injury Intensive Monitoring System." *British Medical Journal* 3:334-6. London.

Fergusson, D.M., Fleming, J., and O'Neill, D.P. 1972. *Child Abuse in New Zealand. A Report on a Nationwide Survey of the Physical Ill-Treatment of Children in New Zealand.* Wellington, N.Z.: A.R. Shearer, Government Printer.

Field, M.H. and Field, H.F. 1973. "Marital Violence and the Criminal Process: Neither Justice nor Peace." *Social Service Review* 47:221-40.

Flynn, W.R. 1970. "Frontier Justice: A Contribution to the Theory of Child Battery." *American Journal of Psychiatry* 127:375-9.

Forrest, T. 1974. "The Family Dynamics of Maternal Violence." *Journal of the American Academy of Psychoanalysis* 2:215-30.

Gelles, R.J. 1973. "Child Abuse as Psychopathology: A Sociological Critique and Reformation." *American Journal of Orthopsychiatry* 43:611-21.

George, J.E. 1973. "Spare the Rod: A Survey of the Battered-Child Syndrome." *Forensic Science* 2:129-67.

Gibbens, T.C.N. 1972. "Violence to Children." *Howard Journal of Penology and Crime Prevention* 13:212-20.

Gil, D.G. 1970. *Violence Against Children: Physical Child Abuse in the United States.* Cambridge, Mass.: Harvard University Press.

———. 1971. "A Sociocultural Perspective on Physical Child Abuse." *Child Welfare* 50:389-95.

Glazier, A.E., ed. 1971. *Child Abuse: A Community Challenge.* East Aurora, N.Y.: Henry Stewart.

Harris, M.J. 1970. "Discussion on the 'Battered Child Syndrome,'" *Australian Journal of Forensic Sciences* 3:77-78. Sydney.

Helfer, R.E. and Kempe, C.H. 1974. *The Battered Child.* 2nd edition. Chicago: University of Chicago Press.

Hoshino, G. and Yoder, G.H. 1973. "Administrative Discretion in the Implementation of Child Abuse Legislation." *Child Welfare* 52:414-24.

Isaacs, S. 1972. "Neglect, Cruelty and Battering." *British Medical Journal* 3:224-26. London.

Jackson, G. 1972. "Child Abuse Syndrome: The Cases We Miss." *British Medical Journal* 2:756-7. London.

Katz, J. 1970. "The Battered Child Syndrome." *Australian Journal of Forensic Sciences* 3:71-76. Sydney.

Kempe, C.H. and Helfer, R.E., eds. 1972. *Helping the Battered Child and His Family*. Philadelphia: J.B. Lippincott.

Langshaw, W.C. 1970. "The Battered Child." *Australian Journal of Forensic Sciences* 3:60-70. Sydney.

"Medical Progress Has Little Effect on an Ancient Childhood Syndrome." 1972. *Journal of the American Medical Association* 222:1605-12.

Melnick, B. and Hurley, J.R. 1969. "Distinctive Personality Attributes of Child Abusing Mothers." *Journal of Consulting Clinical Psychology* 33:746-9.

Nichamin, S.J. 1973. "Battered Child Syndrome and Brain Dysfunction." *Journal of the American Medical Association* 223:1390.

Nixon, H.H. and Court, S.D.M. 1973. "Non-Accidental Injury in Children. Introductory Comment from B.P.S. and B.A.P.S." *British Medical Journal* 4:656-7. London.

Oliver, J.E. and Cox, J. 1973. "A Family Kindred with Ill-Used Children: The Burden on the Community." *British Journal of Psychiatry* 123:81-90. London.

Parnas, R.P. 1971. "Police Discretion and Diversion of Incidents of Intra-Family Violence." *Law and Contemporary Problems* 36:539-65.

_____. 1973. "Prosecutorial and Judicial Handling of Family Violence." *Criminal Law Bulletin* 9:733-69.

Raffalli, H.C. 1970. "The Battered Child: An Overview of a Medical, Legal and Social Problem." *Crime and Delinquency* 16:139-50.

Sattin, D.B. and Miller, J.K. 1971. "The Ecology of Child Abuse within a Military Community." *American Journal of Orthopsychiatry* 41:675-8.

Sayre, J.W., Foley, F.W., Zingarella, L.S., and Kristal, H.F. 1973. "Community Committee on Child Abuse." *New York State Journal of Medicine* 73:2071-75.

Silver, L.B., Dublin, C.C., and Lourier, R.S. 1969. "Does Violence Breed Violence? Contributions from a Study of the Child Abuse Syndrome," *American Journal of Psychiatry* 126:404-7.

_____. 1971. "Agency Action and Interaction in Cases of Child Abuse," *Social Casework* 52:164-71.

Smith, S.M., Hanson, R., and Noble, S. 1973. "Parents of Battered Babies: A Controlled Study." *British Medical Journal* 4:388-91.

Smith, S.M., Honigsberger, L., and Smith, C.H. 1973. "E.E.G. and Personality Factors in Baby Batterers." *British Medical Journal* 3:20-22. London.

Somerhausen, C. 1972. "La Protection des Enfants Martyrs" ["Protection of Maltreated Children"]. *Revue de Droit Pénal et Criminologie* 52:1084-90. Brussels.

Steigard, J. 1970. "The Battered Child Syndrome," *Australian Journal of Forensic Sciences* 3:57-59. Sydney.

Steinmetz, S.K. and Straus, M.A., eds. 1974. *Violence in the Family*. New York: Dodd, Mead and Co.

Straus, M.A. 1973. "General Systems Theory Approach to a Theory of Violence between Family Members." *Social Science Information* 12:105-25.

_____. 1974. "Leveling, Civility, and Violence in the Family." *Journal of Marriage and the Family* 36:13-29.

Terr, L.C. 1970. "A Family Study of Child Abuse." *American Journal of Psychiatry* 127:665-71.

Trube-Becker, E. 1972. "Schweigepflicht und Zeugnisver weigerungsrecht des Arztes bei Delikten gegen das Kind" ["The Doctor's Pledge of Secrecy and His Right as a Witness to Refuse to Answer in Offenses against Children"]. *Münchener Medizinische Wochenschrift* 114:389-92. Munich.

U.S. Department of Health, Education and Welfare. Social and Rehabilitation Service. 1969. *Bibliography on the Battered Child*. Revised edition. Washington, D.C.: U.S. Government Printing Office.

Van Stolk, M. 1972. *The Battered Child in Canada*. Toronto: McClellan and Stewart Ltd.

Viano, E. 1973. *The Battered Child: A Review of Studies and Research in the Area of Child Abuse*. Paper presented at the First International Symposium on Victimology, 2-6 September 1973, Jerusalem. Institute of Criminology, Hebrew University of Jerusalem.

"Violence and the Family." 1971. *Journal of Marriage and the Family* 33:624-731.

"Violent Parents." 1971. *Lancet* 2:1017-8.

Webb, J. et al. 1973. "Non-Accidental Injury in Children: A Guide in Management." *British Medical Journal* 4:657-60. London.

Zurcher, J.C. 1972. *Identifying the Battered or Molested Child. A Handbook for School Staff Members*. Palo Alto: Palo Alto Unified School District.

Drug-Induced Violence

Drug-induced violence can mean violence committed as a result of being under the influence of drugs (or alcohol) or violence committed to support a drug habit.

Considering the enormous amount of literature written on drugs and on violence, it is curious that such a small proportion addresses itself to the interrelationship between the two. This suggests that either proven drug-induced violence does not in itself contribute a significant enough amount to the overall volume of violence in our society to merit special attention, or that no scientifically valid methods have yet been devised for determining and measuring the possible causal relationship between drugs and violence. The latter hypothesis finds support in the Technical Papers of the Second Report of the National Commission on Marihuana and Drug Abuse, which states that "there is little information on specific mechanisms whereby these drugs influence human behavior, particularly the aggressive forms of human behavior involved in crime" (p. 243 of the report, cited here under Tinklenberg). Furthermore, "establishing direct relationships between drug use and crime is extremely difficult. . . . Most of the available data on drug use is unsubstantiated by chemical testing (with the notable exception of the Eckerman study). The data that rely on self-reporting or inferences for drug use at the time of the crime are not valid for formulating clearcut evidence" (p. 246, Tinklenberg). However, in spite of the lack of scientific proof, there seems to be a substantial number of people who are convinced of the causal relationship between drugs and violence.

Advena, J.C. 1974. *Drug Abuse Bibliography for 1972.* Troy, N.Y.: Whitston Publishers.
Baden, M.M. 1972. "Homicide, Suicide, and Accidental Death Among Narcotic Addicts." *Human Pathology* 3:91-95.
Blumberg, H.H. 1973. "Violence among Attenders at a London Drug Clinic." *British Journal of Psychiatry* 122:619.
Borus, J.F. 1973. "Reentry: II. 'Making It' Back in the States." *American Journal of Psychiatry* 130:850-4.
Chiozza, G. and Bandinit, T. 1970. "Indagnini Medico-Legali in Tema di Violenza Carnale Presunta per Inferiorità Psichica da Assunziones di Bevande Alcooliche" ["A Medico-Legal Study of Sexual Violence Precipitated by Mental Inferiority due to Consumption of Alcoholic Beverages"] . *Rassegna di Criminologia* 1:77-84. Genoa.
Cockett, R. 1971. *Drug Abuse and Personality in Young Offenders.* London: Butterworths.
Crick, B.C., ed. 1974. *Crime, Rape and Gin.* Buffalo, N.Y.: Prometheus Books.
Cull, J.G. and Harely, R.E. 1974. *Types of Drug Abusers and Their Users.* Springfield, Ill.: C.C. Thomas.
DuPont, R.L. and Katon, R.N. 1971. "Development of a Heroin-Addiction Treatment Program: Effect on Urban Crime." *Journal of the American Medical Association* 216:1320-4.
Eckerman, W.C., Bates, J.D., Rachel, J.V., and Poole, W.K. 1971. *Drug Usage and Arrest Charges: A Study of Drug Usage and Arrest Charges Amongst Arrestees in Six Metropolitan Areas in the United States.* Bureau of Narcotics and Dangerous Drugs, U.S. Department of Justice. Washington, D.C.: U.S. Government Printing Office.

Ellinwood, E.H. 1971. "Assault and Homicide Associated with Amphetamine Abuse." *American Journal of Psychiatry* 127:1170-5.

Gelfand, M. 1971. "The Extent of Alcohol Consumption by Africans. The Significance of the Weapon at Beer Drinks." *Journal of Forensic Medicine* 18:53-64. Johannesburg.

Gibbens, T.C.N. and Silberman, M. 1970. "Alcoholism among Prisoners." *Psychological Medicine* 1:73-78. London.

Goode, E. 1972. "Marijuana Use and Crime." In National Commission on Marihuana and Drug Abuse, *Marihuana: A Signal of Misunderstanding.* Washington, D.C.: U.S. Government Printing Office.

Goodwin, D.W. 1973. "Alcohol in Suicide and Homicide." *Quarterly Journal of Studies on Alcohol* 34:144-56.

Goodwin, D.W., Crane, J.B., and Guze, S.B. 1971. "Felons Who Drink: An 8-Year Follow-Up." *Quarterly of Studies on Alcohol* 32:136-47.

Hollis, W.S. 1974. "On the Etiology of Criminal Homicides—The Alcohol Factor." *Journal of Police Science and Administration* 2:50-53.

Klepfisz, A. and Racy, J. 1973. "Homicide and LSD." *Journal of the American Medical Association* 223:429-30.

Leavitt, F. 1974. *Drugs and Behavior.* Philadelphia: W.B. Saunders Co.

Lindelius, R. and Salum, I. 1973. "Alcoholism and Criminality." *Acta Psychiatrica Scandinavica* 49:306-14.

Medina, E.L. 1970. "The Role of Alcohol in Accidents and Violence." In R.E. Popham, ed. *Alcohol and Alcoholism.* Toronto: University of Toronto Press.

Miller, L. and Einstein, S. eds. 1972. *Drug Abuse and Social Issues.* White Plains, N.Y.: Albert J. Phiebig.

National Institute of Mental Health. U.S. Department of Health, Education and Welfare. 1973. *Drug Use in America: Problem in Perspective*, 4 Volumes. Technical Papers of the 2nd Report of the National Commission on Marihuana and Drug Abuse. Washington, D.C.: U.S. Government Printing Office.

Nicol, A.R., Gun, J.C., Gristwood, J., Foggitt, R.H., and Watson, J.P. 1973. "The Relationship of Alcoholism to Violent Behavior Resulting in Long-Term Imprisonment." *British Journal of Psychiatry* 123:47-51. London.

Reich, P. and Hepps, R.B. 1972. "Homicide During a Psychosis Induced by LSD." *Journal of the American Medical Association* 219:869-71.

Thum, D., Wechsler, H., and Demone, H.W., Jr. 1973. "Alcohol Levels of Emergency Service Patients Injured in Fights and Assaults." *Criminology* 10:487-97.

Tinklenberg, J. 1973. "Drugs and Crime." In National Institute of Mental Health, *Drug Use in America: Problem in Perspective, Appendix*, Vol. I. Technical Papers of the 2nd Report of the National Commission on Marihuana and Drug Abuse. Washington, D.C.: U.S. Government Printing Office.

Tinklenberg, J. and Stillman, R.C. 1973. "Alcohol and Violence." In P. Bourne and R. Fox, eds., *Alcoholism: Progress in Research and Treatment.* New York: Academic Press.

Warkentin, H. and Osterhaus, E. 1969. "Untersuchungen über Gewalttäter unter Alkoholeinfluss und deren Belastung mit Vorstrafen und Vorgängen ähnlicher Deliktarten" ["Studies on Aggression under the Influence of Alcohol, with Reference to Previous Convictions and Proceedings for Similar Offenses"]. *Kriminalistik* 23:417-20. Hamburg.

U.S. House of Representatives. Select Committee on Crime. 1971. *Amphetamines.* Washington, D.C.: U.S. Government Printing Office.

Compensation to Victims of Violent Crimes

As a final section of this bibliography on violence, it is not inappropriate to include some literature about the hapless victim of violence.[c] The role a victim plays in a criminal act has become an important concern of criminologists in the last few decades, after years of neglect and only perfunctory interest. This increased interest in victims is reflected in the vast and ever-expanding amount of literature now available on the subject.

However, this section of the bibliography will limit itself to only a few references to general works on victimology and will be concerned mainly with society's response to the plight of innocent victims of violent crimes: government-enacted victim compensation programs.

The first program to compensate victims of crime was put into effect by the New Zealand Government in 1964 and subsequently others were set up elsewhere, including in some of the United States. The works presented in this section deal with the basic concepts of victim compensation, the problems it faces or has faced in different jurisdictions, and the experience of those programs that are already in operation.

"Agreements Signed for Federal Support for Legal Aid: Victim's Compensation." 1973. *Canadian Bar Association Journal* 4:5-7.

"Awards of the Crimes Compensation Board." 1970. *Saskatchewan Law Review* 35:75-76.

Brooks, J. 1973a. "Compensating Victims of Crime: The Recommendations of Program Administrators." *Law and Society Review* 7:445-71.

_____. 1973b. "Crime Compensation Programs: An Opinion Survey of Program Administrators." *Criminology* 11:258-74.

[c]N.B.: Recently compiled bibliographies on this subject already exist in two new publications that should be referred to for additional citations. See pages 245 to 250 in Drapkin and Viano, *Victimology*, cited in this section and pages 294 and 302 in Edelhertz and Geis, *Public Compensation to Victims of Crime*, also cited here.

Chappell, D. 1970. "The Emergence of Australian Schemes to Compensate Victims of Crime." *Southern California Law Review* 43:69-83.

_____. 1972. "Providing for the Victim of Crime: Political Placebos or Progressive Programs?" *Adelaide Law Review* 4:294-306. South Australia.

Coon, T.E. 1971. "Public Defender and Victims' Compensation Legislation: Their Part in the Criminal Justice System." *Police* 16:18-20.

"Criminal Victim Compensation in Maryland." 1970. *Maryland Law Review* 30:266-83.

Drapkin, I. and Viano, E., eds. 1974. *Victimology*. Lexington, Mass.: Lexington Books.

_____. Forthcoming. *Victimology: A New Focus*, 5 Volumes. Includes papers presented at the First International Symposium on Victimology, 2-6 September 1973, Jerusalem. Lexington, Mass.: Lexington Books.

Drobny, P.J. 1971. "Compensation to Victims of Crime: An Analysis." *St. Louis University Law Journal* 16:201-17.

Edelhertz, H. and Geis, G. 1974. *Public Compensation to Victims of Crime*. New York: Praeger Publishers.

Edelhertz, H., Geis, G., Chappell, D., and Sutton, L.P. 1973. "Public Compensation of Victims of Crime: A Survey of the New York Experience." *Criminal Law Bulletin* 9:5-47 (Part I); 9:101-23 (Part II).

Floyd, G.E. 1972. "Victim Compensation: A Comparative Study." *Trial* 8:14-16, 18-19, 27.

Geis, G. 1970. "Victims of Violent Crime: Should They Be Compensated?" *Vital Issues* 20:1-4.

Geis, G. and Edelhertz, H. 1974. "California's New Crime Victim Compensation Statute." *San Diego Law Review* 11:880-905.

Geis, G. and Weiner, R.A. 1970. "International Conference on Compensation to Innocent Victims of Crime." *International Review of Criminal Policy* 26:123-5.

Hook, S. 1972. "The Rights of the Victims: Thoughts on Crime and Compassion." *Encounter* 38:11-15.

Jacob, B.R. 1970. "Reparation or Restitution by the Criminal Offender to His Victim: Applicability of an Ancient Concept in the Modern Correctional Process." *Journal of Criminal Law, Criminology and Police Science* 61:152-7.

Kelman, H.C. 1973. "Violence Without Moral Restraint: Reflections on Dehumanization of Victims and Victimizers." *Journal of Social Issues* 29:25-61.

Kitunen, K. 1971. *Vahingankorvaus väkivaltarikollisuudess* [*Compensation to Victims of Crimes of Violence*]. Series M:10. Helsinki: Institute of Criminology.

Kutner, L. 1972. "Crime Torts: Due Process for Crime Victims." *Trial* 8:28-30.

Lamborn, L.L. 1973a. "The Propriety of Governmental Compensation of Victims of Crime." *George Washington Law Review* 41:446-70.

_____. 1973b. "The Scope of Programs for Governmental Compensation of Victims of Crime." *University of Illinois Law Reform* 1973:21-87.

Laster, R.E. 1970. "Criminal Restitution: A Survey of Its Past History, and an Analysis of Its Present Usefulness." *University of Richmond Law Review* 5:1971-98.

McClellan, J.L. 1972. "Victims of Crime Act of 1972: Society's Moral Obligation." *Trial* 8:22-24.

Mansfield, M.J. 1972. "Justice for the Victims of Crime." *Houston Law Review* 9:75-80.

Nordenson, U.K. 1972. "The Proposed Swedish Systems of Free Legal Assistance and of Compensation to Victims of Crime." *Journal of Legal Medicine* 70:103-8.

Quinney, R. 1972. "Who is the Victim?" *Criminology* 10:314-23.

_____. 1973. "Rehabilitation of the Victims of Crime: An Overview." *U.C.L.A. Law Review* 21:317-70.

Schafer, S. 1970. "Victim Compensation and Responsibility." *Southern California Law Review* 43:55-67.

_____. 1972. "Corrective Compensation." *Trial* 8:25-27.

Schultz, L.G. 1972. "A Compensation Program for Sex Victims." In H.L. Gochros and L.G. Schultz, eds., *Human Sexuality and Social Work.* New York: Association Press.

Shank, W. 1970. "Aid to Victims of Violent Crimes in California." *Southern California Law Review* 43:85-92.

Van Rensselaer, S.L. 1972. "A Compensation Board at Work." *Trial* 8:20-21.

Weeks, K.M. 1970. "The New Zealand Criminal Injuries Compensation Scheme." *Southern California Law Review* 43:107-21.

Williams, D.B. 1972. *Criminal Injuries Compensation.* London: Oyez Publishing.

Yarborough, R.W. 1970. "The Battle for a Federal Violent Crimes Compensation Act: The Genesis of S.9." *Southern California Law Review* 43:93-106.

About the Editors

Duncan Chappell is the director of the Law and Justice Study Center of Battelle Memorial Institute in Seattle, Washington and an affiliate member of the Department of Sociology at the University of Washington. He received the LL.B from the University of Tasmania in 1962 and the Ph.D. in criminal law and criminology from the University of Cambridge in 1965. He was associate professor of Criminal Justice at the School of Criminal Justice, State University of New York at Albany from 1971 to 1973 and has acted as consultant to various universities and research organizations. He is presently consultant to the United States Senate Select Committee on Small Business (Criminal Redistribution Systems). Dr. Chappell is coauthor of the book *The Police and the Public in Australia and New Zealand* (1969), coeditor of the comprehensive volume *The Australian Criminal Justice System* (1972), and has published widely in journals of criminology and law in Australia, the United States, and England.

John Monahan received the B.A. from the State University of New York at Stony Brook in 1968 and the Ph.D. in clinical psychology from Indiana University in 1972. He is currently an assistant professor in the crossdisciplinary program in Social Ecology at the University of California, Irvine. Dr. Monahan is a frequent contributor to journals in the fields of psychology, psychiatry, and law and is on the editorial staffs of the *American Journal of Community Psychology* and *Criminal Justice and Behavior*. He is the editor of *Community Mental Health and the Criminal Justice System*.